T0054909

The British Empire: A Very Short Introduction

VERY SHORT INTRODUCTIONS are for anyone wanting a stimulating and accessible way in to a new subject. They are written by experts, and have been published in more than 25 languages worldwide.

The series began in 1995, and now represents a wide variety of topics in history, philosophy, religion, science, and the humanities. The VSI Library now contains more than 300 volumes—a Very Short Introduction to everything from ancient Egypt and Indian philosophy to conceptual art and cosmology—and will continue to grow in a variety of disciplines.

Very Short Introductions available now:

For more information visit our website
www.oup.com/vsi/

Ashley Jackson

THE BRITISH EMPIRE

A Very Short Introduction

OXFORD
UNIVERSITY PRESS

OXFORD
UNIVERSITY PRESS

Great Clarendon Street, Oxford, ox2 6DP,
United Kingdom

Oxford University Press is a department of the University of Oxford.
It furthers the University's objective of excellence in research, scholarship,
and education by publishing worldwide. Oxford is a registered trade mark of
Oxford University Press in the UK and in certain other countries

First Edition published in 2013

British Library Cataloguing in Publication Data

Data available

ISBN 978-0-19-960541-5

Printed and bound by
CPI Group (UK) Ltd, Croydon, CR0 4YY

This book is dedicated to my wonderful grandmother, Pauline Vivienne Townshend, with my love and devotion

Acknowledgements

This book has benefited incalculably from the advice of two anonymous OUP readers, one an internal editor, the other an external academic. I have adopted their suggestions wholesale as they will see, and attempted to respond thoroughly to their well-aimed criticisms. Despite their efforts, however, a 'council of perfection' (to borrow one of their phrases) has not been achieved. But hopefully the minefield has been more successfully navigated than I would have managed alone, though not, it is anticipated, without some detonations. Thanks are also due to Emma Ma and Luciana O'Flaherty at OUP, to Julia Engelhardt for her excellent work on the images, to Lelaytha Chattukutty of the History Department, National University of Singapore, for so kindly printing versions of the manuscript during my stay there, to Edwin Pritchard for his copyediting expertise, to David Tomkins and to my wife, Andrea, for her constant encouragement.

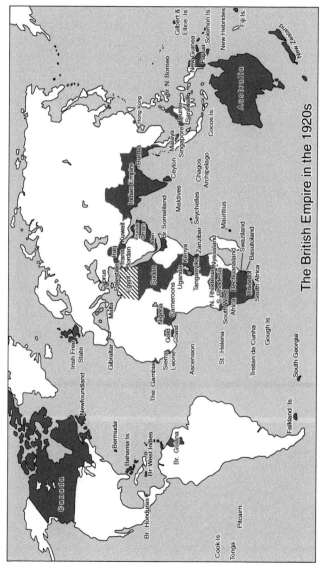

The British Empire in the 1920s

1. A map of the British Empire

Contents

Preface

Sometimes books about the British Empire ask more questions than they offer answers. They emphasize the complexity of the subject and tour its historiographical trenches rather than providing firm handholds that readers new to the subject can grip as they ascend the British Empire's many-branched tree of knowledge. This prudent approach reflects the enormity of the subject—which at its broadest amounts to the history of a quarter of the world over the course of several centuries—and the diverse and sometimes conflicting histories that it has produced. But hedging with the subject's complexity and heterogeneity can leave the reader feeling rudderless.

The approach taken here has been to pose questions and then to attempt to provide answers in order to present a relatively hard-edged picture of the British Empire. It is hoped that this approach will leave readers new to the subject in a position to move on and discover for themselves its richness and its manifold nuances and competing interpretations (on even the most basic questions, such as what caused imperial expansion, the extent to which the British public was influenced by possession of a vast empire, or whether indeed such a thing as the British Empire even existed!). The book attempts to assess whether the British Empire was a good thing or a bad thing—treacherous terrain that imperial historians often shun—because contemporary coverage of the Empire so often appears wrapped in this debate, and because it is a natural question for anyone interested in the subject to ask.

This approach has been adopted in order to avoid the alternative; an array of caveats and disclaimers accompanying each assertion, and the dancing on pinheads that often attends reviews of the subject's major historiographical debates. The text inevitably reflects its author's background, strengths, and weaknesses. Yet in an effort to reassure the reader that this is not an unreliable maverick's manifesto, it should be said that the text corresponds in general with the major publications on the British Empire, such as the multi-authored *Oxford History of the British Empire* and the most important single-volume histories published in recent years.

List of illustrations

Introduction

The expansion of Europe was one of the most significant
phenomena to shape the modern world. Munshi Abdullah,
witnessing the transformation wrought by colonization in 1840s
Singapore, wrote: 'I am astonished to see how markedly our world
is changing. A new world is being created, the old world
destroyed. The very jungle becomes a settled district while
elsewhere a settlement reverts to jungle.' Pioneered in the modern
age by the Iberian powers of Portugal and Spain, vociferously
pursued by the Dutch, French, and Russians, taken up late by the
Americans, Belgians, Germans, Italians, and Japanese, global
colonization became the special preserve of the British.

At its height, the British Empire comprised over 13,000,000
square miles-nearly one-quarter of the earth's land surface-and its
merchant marine and navy were supreme at sea. Following the
acquisition of new colonies in Africa, the Middle East, and the
Pacific in the wake of the First World War, Britain was responsible
for ruling 500 million people, over a fifth of the earth's population.
Measured on indicators of power such as political, economic,
and strategic reach, the British Empire was the world's sole
superpower. It retained this position until the Second World War,
a conflict that accelerated trends that were already making the
possession of colonies increasingly anachronistic and diminishing

Britain's (and Europe's) standing in the international system. These economic, political, and cultural trends, and the dramatic changes caused by prolonged global conflict and a rising tide of nationalism, led to the demise of the British Empire during a decolonization spree that witnessed the birth of scores of new nation-states in the four decades following 1945. The aberration that had been Europe's 'moment' of global pre-eminence, in which Britain had been to the fore, had passed.

Long after its demise, the British Empire remains a controversial topic. In 2009 Ayatollah Ali Khamenei identified 'evil' Britain as the foremost enemy of the Islamic Republic of Iran, plumbing a rich vein of anti-British sentiment rooted in imperial interventions dating back to the nineteenth century. In 2005, President Thabo Mbeki of South Africa lambasted British imperialists such as Winston Churchill who had travelled to Africa and Asia 'doing terrible things wherever they went'. In 2007 an American author published a book entitled *The Evil Empire: 101 Ways in Which England Ruined the World*, whilst five years later *All the Countries We've Ever Invaded* claimed that the British had put in a hostile appearance in 90 per cent of the world's countries at one time or another.

In Britain, anything to do with the Empire raises temperatures as well as headlines (though perhaps giving a measure of the Empire's diminishing significance and the capacity of post-colonial societies to 'move on', this is less often the case in former colonies). In 2011 a statue of the explorer Henry Morton Stanley was erected in his home town in Wales, to great controversy. Was Stanley to be celebrated still as a hero of Victorian exploration, or pilloried for his excesses and for his role in opening Africa to pernicious European influences? In 2009 Cambridge University was accused of advocating slavery and racism by hosting an 'Empire Ball' in honour of 'the Victorian Commonwealth and all its decadences'. Whilst revellers were exhorted to 'party like it's 1899', protestors pointed to slavery, concentration camps, and a legacy of racial division.

Apologies for, or assertions about its beneficence, define coverage of the British Empire and its legacies in the former 'mother country' and elsewhere. 'Did Britain Wreck the World?' asked a *Newsweek* headline in 2011, whilst a *Financial Times* article appeared under the title 'The Guilt and the Glory'. Michael Palin, President of the Royal Geographical Society, claimed that the British Empire was not as 'wicked' as it was often portrayed, and urged Britons to stop apologizing for their colonial past. British Prime Minister Gordon Brown made the same plea whilst visiting a former African colony in 2005, claiming that 'great British values' such as freedom, tolerance, and civic duty could be admired as some of the country's most successful exports. Apparently a rite of passage for British leaders, his successor David Cameron told an audience in Pakistan that Britain was to blame for many of the world's problems, sparking a flurry of 'was the Empire good or bad?' coverage in the British media. The release in 2011 of thousands of previously withheld British government files saw academic and media attention focus on alleged British atrocities during colonial insurgencies of the 1950s, augmented by a High Court case between Mau Mau victims and the British government (won by the former in 2012). In turn, this coverage elicited a doughty defence of the imperial record. Of course mistakes were made, wrote the historian Lawrence James in the *Daily Mail*, ploughing a familiar furrow, 'but we must never stop being proud of the Empire', which spread progress, stability, and beneficial institutions.

Why the controversy? Because any study of imperialism embraces a range of controversial topics, including unequal power relations, nationalism, race, cultural confrontations, economics, warfare, and ideology. It is controversial because the British Empire affected so many countries in lasting ways and epitomized a period in which, all around the world, non-Europeans were dominated by Europeans. The Empire shaped the modern world, from place names and geographical boundaries to racial demographics, economic networks, and international norms and laws. It was the major force in the creation of a coherent international order and a potent agent of globalization. The Empire is also controversial because something as large defies easy summary, and perspectives on it vary wildly. It is possible for its admirers or detractors to cherry-pick examples to 'prove' that British rule, overall, was either good or bad, its legacies beneficent or diabolical. Some argue that it was an engine of modernization, others that it was a vehicle of exploitation. As the headlong decolonization of the European empires gathered pace in the 1960s, Jean-Paul Sartre wrote that 'We in Europe too are being decolonized. The settler which is in every one of us is being savagely rooted out… It was nothing but an ideology of lies, a perfect justification for pillage; its honeyed words, its affectation of sensibility were only alibis for our aggressions.' Coming from an entirely different camp in a different age, in the early twenty-first century the historian Niall Ferguson argued that the British Empire was better than the other empires of the period. Though its record was by no means untarnished, it brought beneficial global trade and the rule of law, and was overwhelmingly a force for stability and good, influences conspicuously lacking in contemporary badland regions where empire had once held sway.

At its most easily grasped level, the British Empire was a collection of overseas territories governed by offices of the British state or its representatives, though the degree of control varied as did the space in which indigenous people could retain a measure of autonomy. Furthermore, British rule always rested not only upon British military, political, and economic power, but upon alliance with indigenous leaders, elites, and the many indigenous people who were employed by the colonial state. From the eighteenth century until the 1950s it was the world's largest political entity, a powerful military and strategic alliance, and an economic bloc. Of the world's 203 nation states, sixty-three were once ruled by Britain. About twenty others were occupied by Britain for briefer periods, including Cuba, Eritrea, Greece, Guadeloupe, Indonesia, Libya, Madagascar, Martinique, the

Philippines, Senegal, Spain, and Vietnam. At least seven more can be counted as having formed part of Britain's 'informal' empire, a term used to denote a country not officially ruled by Britain but so influenced by it that a patron–client relationship pertained and Britain exercised a disproportionate influence upon the country's rulers and its economy. These countries include Argentina, Chile, parts of maritime China, and Iran. Thus around a third of the world's nation-states at one point or another experienced British rule or significant British influence.

The territories that formed the British Empire—a word meaning sovereignty over a group of nations or peoples—ranged from tiny islands to vast segments of the world's major continents, especially Africa, the Americas, Antarctica, Asia, and Australasia. Stretched across each ocean and time zone, the proud claim that 'the sun never set on the British Empire' was actually true (some said that this was because the British could not be trusted in the dark). Until the 1950s the hackneyed sun-never-set phrase was a commonplace of boys' adventure comics and advertisements for products as diverse as Bird's custard powder and Craven tobacco, illustrating the manner in which themes relating to empire and the non-European world, and Britain's exulted place within it, penetrated British culture and contributed to the formation of an inchoate but powerful imperial mind-set and a sense of British superiority and fitness to rule other peoples.

Visual depictions of the Empire's geographical extent were regularly encountered by British people and British subjects overseas, reflecting nationalism, 'race patriotism', and an emergent pride in the creation of a British-shaped world order, a veritable British world. Most commonly, this was through maps of the world centred on the British Isles and showing imperial possessions shaded in red, connected by oceanic trade routes, underwater telegraph cables, and a chain of coaling stations—all, of course, British. It was an iconic representation of global power, encountered in school classrooms and atlases the world over as

2. Empire Marketing Board poster 1927–1933, 'Highways of Empire'.
The EMB was formed to stimulate the British and imperial economy,
particularly by persuading people to 'buy imperial'. The British map of
the world, reflecting the Empire's maritime and commercial character
and geographical range, was a powerful national boast. A wide range of
ephemera and more durable media and objects transmitted ideas
about the privileged place of Britain (and Britons) in relation to other
lands and their peoples. British coins, for instance, bore the monarch's
image and the Latin inscription 'King of all the Britains; Emperor of
India'

well as in posters, souvenir brochures, and on day-to-day objects
such as stamps, ashtrays, and matchboxes. The Diamond Match
Company's 'Empire Match' bore a red-shaded world map and the
legend 'We hold a vaster Empire than has been'. A 1902 advert for
Bovril featured each letter of the product's name made up of the
map outlines of dozens of colonies. And so on. Meanwhile,
Britain's domination of the map was used by its rivals to pillory
British imperialism. French, German, and Italian cartoonists
represented Britain variously as a serpent constricting the globe,
as a hideous claw-like hand grasping it, and as an obese John Bull
with the red-dominated map spread across his girth. As well as
using Britain's global position to censure it, such responses

reflected a potent national jealousy in an age where other powers were increasingly yearning for their own 'place in the sun'. With their pith-helmets and 'Bombay bloomers' (a name for baggy shorts), British imperialists were an easy target for the caricaturist, 'nasty, brutish, and in shorts', to borrow Brian Aldiss's play on Thomas Hobbes' phrase. But there were other, more benign visions of Britain's empire too – and not just those conjured by the British themselves.

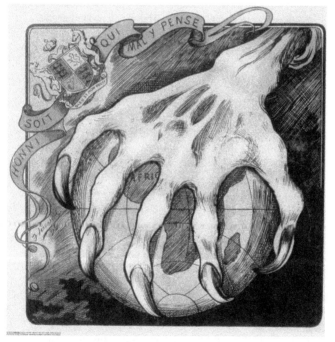

3. A French caricature of British imperialism, 1899: A claw-like hand encompasses the earth with the wording of the Royal Arms ironically displayed: 'Honi soit qui mal y pense (shame on him who thinks ill of it)'. A powerful image, typical of anti-British illustrations in foreign media

The palpable existence of a British world was felt by Britons and foreigners alike. It was part of the furniture of the international order, with a degree of permanency about it belied by its sudden collapse following the Second World War. In 1938 Enoch Powell flew from Britain to Sydney by Imperial Airways flying-boat to take up the chair of Greek at Sydney University.

> Those sixteen days from Poole Harbour to Sydney were a deeply formative experience...It was an exacting routine. Three or four times a day, the flying-boat landed on a sheet of water – lake or river or sea...The traveller of 1938 saw the world close to. It was an incomparable geography lesson – and largely a lesson in Imperial geography. Between Crete and Indonesia there was only one stop out of almost a score – it was, in fact, Bangkok – where the flying-boat touched down anywhere not under British rule or effectively under British authority. Alexandria, the Lake of Galilee, Habbaniya, Basra, Abu Dhabi, Mekran, Karachi, Jaipur, Allahabad, Calcutta, Akyab, Rangoon, Penang, Singapore – one was witnessing the ubiquity of a power on which the sun had not yet set.

The American journalist Cecil Brown remarked upon exactly the same phenomenon on a journey from Egypt to Singapore: 'For five days of flying, from Suez to Singapore, at almost every stop we had touched on water under the protection of the British flag. It was a stunning reflection on Empire.' The memoirs of both men evoke the lost world of the British Empire, and convey a sense of the geography—the imperial geography—that pertained until the 1960s when, with astonishing speed, the Empire dissolved and Britain reverted to an earlier incarnation as a medium-sized European nation, with a global outlook but without a global empire.

As well as describing its physical and political dimensions, the term 'the British Empire' encompassed a collection of projects organized in Britain and its overseas colonies, projects aimed at securing profit for the principals or otherwise forwarding their interests, interests sometimes construed as embracing those of

4. A British world: From the reign of George VI, a stamp from the British Solomon Islands. In the colonies, postage stamps showed local scenes—Lake Naivasha, Grand Harbour Valletta, the Victoria Falls—or local industries such as orange cultivation and teak forestry, all watched over by a portrait of the British king or queen. Alternatively, colonial stamps would bear images of Britain, such as royal coronations, castles, or the Houses of Parliament

indigenous peoples too (perhaps by 'civilizing' them, or bringing the apparent boon of Western education and justice, or preventing them from fighting each other, all powerful elements in contemporary justifications of empire). It was also a collection of state projects conducted in competition with other states. The impressive expansion of the British Empire between the seventeenth and nineteenth centuries depended on Europe's technological resources, and on Britain's success in preventing European challengers from establishing themselves as it came to the forefront of a Western-dominated global economic and political system. The Empire was a product of the rise of global capitalism, an international order underwritten by Britain until replaced by America in the twentieth century. The Empire's decline and fall reflected the eclipse of Europe by superpowers and supranational bodies such as the United Nations, and the rise of anti-colonial ideas and the activities of nationalists and freedom fighters no longer prepared to tolerate European rule.

The British Empire shaped the destinies of the hundreds of millions of people who lived within its bounds. In the settler states of America, Australia, Canada, New Zealand, South Africa, and Southern Rhodesia, white immigrants came to rule the indigenous inhabitants with only minimal control or regulation from Britain itself. Elsewhere, the British parliament, through Whitehall bureaucracies and overseas civil services, were responsible for governance in Aden, Belize, Bengal, Fiji, Gibraltar, Guyana, Hong Kong, Newfoundland, the Maldives, Papua New Guinea, Swaziland, Trinidad, Uganda, Zanzibar, and scores of other colonies. Though indigenous leaders retained sometimes significant measures of autonomy when it came to ruling 'their' people, they did so as subordinates and on behalf of British overlords. Furthermore, it was British institutions, politicians, and governors who were responsible for the 'big things' that define a government's duties. Such things included monetary policy, foreign affairs, taxation, defence and security, constitutional reform, law and order, land policy, road-building, town planning, and the regulation of trade. British officials were able to tax people, claim their labour, and send them to war, telling measures of the extent of imperial power. Augmenting its grip on the Empire, Britain disbursed power in the international system that established the terms governing each colony's interaction with the global economy, mediating each colony's relationship with the wider world and the forces that shaped it. The colonial state might have been small, but its power over people was remarkable; the impact upon people's lives of a deepening encounter with the global economy which it brokered was even more so.

Imperialism's role in brokering global capitalism and deepening Westernization was fundamentally more significant than the

British Empire per se. The eruption across the world of Europeans, and the profound political, social, and economic changes that trailed in their wake, was an epochal process. The coming of imperial influences often meant a significant loss of control over the forces shaping one's life at the level of the individual and the community. Whilst for some well-placed people the coming of British rule or the establishment of a British-controlled port or trading post could be a liberation and source of opportunity, for others it could be catastrophic. There was never a one-size-fits-all colonial experience; depictions of empire that emphasize thralldom, violence, and ruthless exploitation are as hopelessly flawed as those that focus on the rule of law, stability, free trade, and beneficent progress. The calm and relatively liberal character of the late (i.e. twentieth century) Empire should not obscure earlier conditions; whilst it might have appeared peaceful by the twentieth century, this was often because violence in an earlier period had made it so and had entrenched a spectrum of inequality around the globe.

Though the British Empire, and the phenomenon of large territorial empires, might appear curious now, empires have been the default setting throughout human history, which is one of the reasons why accounts that single out the British Empire for special persecution are unbalanced. Man- and womankind of all racial backgrounds have sought to colonize each other in various ways since the dawn of time. The history of empire is far older than the history of the nation-state, and scores of empires have risen and fallen, their size varying from the regional to the global, and the power of their ruling cores to command their extremities differing widely from empire to empire and from age to age. By contrast, today's international system, comprising over 200 sovereign nation-states, is a novelty.

This historic background notwithstanding, it is still possible to view empires as curious structures. The British Empire was curious because it was ectopic, its core manifestation being people who were out of place, people erecting edifices of power and authority that allowed them to influence and even dominate the native inhabitants of lands far from their own and to control their resources—to take over places belonging to *other* people. Britain was a Johnnie-come-lately in the business of empire-building as European great powers explored, ransacked, and subjugated the 'new world', creating potent connections between European 'metropoles' and non-European 'peripheries' that were the foundations of the colonial empires that dominated the international system from the seventeenth until the twentieth century. Yet from its modest early position, dwarfed by other states who had blazed imperial trails around the world, over the course of a century Britain's fortunes waxed, its industry and commerce revolutionized the global economy, and almost everywhere in the world there appeared Britons running up the Union Flag and claiming icepacks and tropical islands for the crown or for some private, 'chartered' company. In the process, like a cuckoo in the nest, Britain eclipsed and supplanted its European rivals and became the world's pre-eminent maritime nation, both in terms of global trade and naval strength, accruing vast colonial holdings in the process and to a significant extent creating the modern world.

Chapter 1
The red on the map

Why Britain?

Before answering the question 'what was the British Empire?' this chapter considers some of the reasons why Britain was in a position to acquire an empire in the first place. European powers were able to conquer distant lands due to a number of factors, including Europe's greater investment in gunpowder technology than other regions. Beyond this, Europe's success was based on conditions such as the existence of similar sized countries and the corresponding absence of a hegemon, together with incessant warfare and the rapid diffusion of innovations. Within this European milieu, Britain's particular success stemmed from the state's early possession of an internal monopoly of violence following the conclusion of civil wars and the defeat of uprisings, the disarmament of nobles, and the integration into a new 'united kingdom' of the Irish and the Scottish. It also experienced significant population increase—from 4.9 million in 1688 to 12 million in 1815—and there grew an abnormally large 'middle class'. Together, these factors meant that there was a rapidly growing domestic market ready to be satisfied by overseas products. There were then the geographical facts of Britain's location, its long coastlines fostering seafaring skills and traditions and early contact with regions such as the Baltic, the Low Countries, and the Iberian peninsula. Island status also provided a significant degree of security against invasion. It became increasingly common for the British to reach beyond Europe, in many ways to attempt to outflank it. Seaborne commerce was at the heart of Britain's evolving relations with the world and its eventual growth as an imperial power. The ocean was a connector rather than a barrier, and long before a British Empire became discernible, British people derived wealth and experience from wool, fishing, and other forms of seagoing engagement beyond the British Isles.

Having considered why Britain was well suited to empire-building, one might ask what was distinctive about the British Empire? Its size and globality was a unique feature; after the First World War, around ninety separate territories owed allegiance to the British crown or were in treaty relations with it. Also unique was its creation of overseas satellites—strong settler societies forged by British emigrants that emitted pulses of imperial energy in their surrounding regions. There was then the incorporation of English, Irish, Scottish, and Welsh people into the business of empire, creating enormous energy in the process. In its early years the extraordinary vigour generated by a range of Protestant denominations vying with each other in missionary endeavour pushed the Empire's boundaries. The British Empire was more individualistic than the centrally controlled, state religion-dominated Catholic empires, its commercial enterprises and chartered companies freer to act unhindered by church or state. Another definitive feature was the shift from an empire of commerce and the sea—the form of empire that dominated in the seventeenth and much of the eighteenth century—to a territorial empire of conquest and settlement. What further marked it out from rival European empires was the impact of Britain's industrialization and the shift from mercantilism to free trade that attended it.

Andrew Thompson further elucidates the attributes that helped generate the momentum for British overseas expansion and the creation of the 'red on the map' British Empire. These included the evolution of a powerful 'fiscal-military' state, one of the largest and most efficient states in the world and one that was in significant ways replicated in India. Two formidable state capacities were developed during wars with France in the late eighteenth and early nineteenth centuries—the capacity to wage war on an unprecedented scale and to levy taxes and borrow money cheaply when required. Another aspect was the spread of racial hierarchies and stereotypes based on the idea of the British being a 'governing race'. Crucial too was the evolution of a laissez-faire state willing to allow British people and institutions to go about their business as a vast and diverse array of groups in British society became caught up in the processes of expansion. The laissez-faire state was also able to cede local governance to settler communities overseas, diminishing the prospect of imperial civil wars such as the American War of Independence, and contributing instead to the forging of settler identities that could be simultaneously British, imperial, and local.

There was then the unprecedented drive for overseas markets as Britain became the first industrialized nation, free trade and the search for investment opportunities becoming signature features of British expansion. Britain was the world's strongest industrial power, and under the discipline of the unregulated market became the workshop of the world. Industrialization transformed the nature of British world power and free trade created a series of satellite economies overseas. As John Darwin writes, it facilitated the global projection of military power far beyond the old limits of wind-powered warships, enabling much greater inland penetration than ever before, and greatly cheapened its use once telegraphs, steamships, and rails could shuttle information and manpower across vast distances. Added to this, ever-longer range rifles, machine-guns, shallow-draft gunboats, and artillery pieces increased lethality. 'It turned the demographic imperialism of settler societies from a slow laborious advance into a blitzkrieg invasion, swamping local resistance and transforming faraway natural environments into new Britains. It hugely reinforced the cultural prestige of the imperial rulers and increased the volume and intensity of their cultural impact.'

Industrialization was also connected to two other preconditions enabling the growth of the British world system—the migration of tens of millions of people and the export of hundreds of millions of pounds sterling. The City of London established itself as the centre of international trade in foodstuffs and raw materials and became a 'strongbox' to invest in. Free trade became 'a form of imperialism that did not, perhaps dare not, speak its name. Equality of access to markets sounded fine in theory; in practice, however, Britain was the country in by far the best position to take advantage of it'. Underpinning this unique system of overseas settlement and commercial relations was the supremacy at sea of the Royal Navy, vital for the growth and security of the British Empire.

> By 1800 [John Darwin writes], British commerce was geared for long distance traffic and the long credit advances required by the cycle of commodity trades; the infrastructure necessary to exercise maritime power in almost every part of the world was in place; and the British consumer was already addicted to a range of exotic new tastes, both cultural and physical. Economic and religious transformation had created a restless, competitive, pluralistic and guilt-ridden society, harbouring rival visions of empire and of Britain's true place in a world needing redemption. It had the means and the motive to widen the bridgeheads already established in the world beyond Europe, and to send in new 'landings' for commerce, conversion, and colonization.

An empire of many peoples

The British Empire comprised diverse peoples as one would expect given its global range. Afrikaner, Arab, Australian, Chinese, Cypriot, Dayak, Igbo, Inuit, Irish, Maasai, Maltese, Pathan, San,

Shona, Sikh, Somali, Tongan, Yoruba, Zulu; this incredible kaleidoscope of peoples and cultures shone within the British Empire. Its most powerful people were on the whole white Britons and other Europeans. For much of its existence it had within its bounds the world's largest Muslim population. The enormous variety of peoples within the British Empire was reflected in the variety of their responses to British imperialism. They were organized in many different ways, from complex states to stateless societies. They were not mere victims of European colonial intrusion, James Belich emphasizes, but also 'intense, courageous, and well-organized' protagonists who often gave as good as they got in resisting British encroachment, until the superior resources of settlers or soldiers overcame them, or they decided that accommodation was more prudent than continued resistance.

Given that it encompassed so many diverse peoples and polities, the British Empire is usefully conceptualized as an *imperial state*. If the Empire is viewed as one would normally view a nation-state, its shape becomes clearer, its existence, to use P. D. Morgan's often-borrowed phrase, as 'one vast interconnected whole', easier to comprehend. There was its capital and heartland, Britain, and its prosperous home counties, the 'white' dominions. Some of its provinces were loosely ruled, others directly administered. Some of its outlying regions were rebellious, their borders frequently contested. Despite marked local variations, it shared many common elements, including bureaucratic and legal practices, civil services, institutions such as police forces, banks, and the monarchy, capital and grant resources, and communication facilities, and was subject to the imperial parliament in all things, in theory if not always in practice. Its bureaucratic, commercial, legal, and military culture was distinctly British though many local varieties occurred. Shifting hybridity on a British framework was the order of the day. Whilst there was a uniformity at the highest levels of imperial rule, pragmatism dictated the 'shape' of imperial rule on the ground, and this meant that local variety was an important part of the picture.

The British Empire used sometimes to be conceived as a sequence of lines extending from Britain out to the manifold areas of empire, but this approach has been abandoned for recognition of complex webs of connections, centred in Britain but also in its major overseas cities and with many reciprocal influences in the other direction. Though on some readings it might have appeared solid, ordered, and hierarchical, the Empire was 'an interconnected zone constituted by multiple points of contact and complex circuits of exchange'. But coherent central power was a defining feature too: whilst the links between distant colonies and bureaucratic and political structures in London might sometimes appear to have been tenuous, they were surprisingly real. London's interest in tiny outposts or apparently empty quarters could become intense if some event caused its gaze to come to rest there. The British imperial style allowed governors to get on with it and run things as they saw fit, with a light touch from London.

The Empire's constituent parts

The Empire was a mass of territories acquired over a period of four centuries, ruled from London with varying degrees of direct and indirect control, and administered on the ground by British appointed civil servants and soldiers, or sometimes employees of British companies. Rule was always exercised with the assistance of indigenous political elites—most pre-colonial, some British created, some powerful, some weak—as well as a host of indigenous employees. Whilst it is often remarked that India was ruled by a small cadre of British civil servants—around about a thousand—what is seldom mentioned in the same breath is that the Government of India employed about a million Indians to assist them in the enterprise. Early imperial rule tended to be quite ad hoc, as it took years for a definable system of administration to develop. The highest imperial authority was the British parliament and the monarch. In the 'white' dominions, settler parliaments also became part of the ruling structure, the passage of their legislative acts dependent upon the approval of the British parliament, their courts subject to the Privy Council in London. Specialist offices of state in Whitehall were responsible for colonial administration, evolving from earlier ad hoc arrangements (for example, the War Office was at one time also responsible for the colonies). They included the Foreign Office, the Colonial Office, the India Office, from the 1920s a Dominions Office, and, briefly, a Burma Office. In turn, specific civil services were established to administer the colonies on the ground, including the Indian Civil Service, the Sudan Political Service, and what in its final years was known as Her Majesty's Overseas Civil Service, responsible for the colonial empire and not formally wound up until 1999. The personnel of private companies such as the British South Africa Company in Southern Rhodesia and the East India Company were also heavily involved in ruling the Empire.

A great deal of effort was invested in projecting imperial authority, displaying its governors and viceroys, marking royal occasions and the annual Empire Day celebrations with elaborate ceremonies, all backed up with displays of the Empire's military capacity, both to reassure and to warn and to make the Empire seem more 'real', powerful, and monolithic than ever in fact it was. The quotidian experience of imperial authority for most of the Empire's people was much less visible. Whilst they might occasionally behold a district commissioner touring his 'reserve', performing his legal functions or supervising the damming of a river, authority and bureaucracy was more often encountered in the guise of chiefs, headmen, 'tribal' policemen, and 'native' clerks, or in India through the person and representatives of a maharajah or nawab or of the powerful landowning elites with whom the British formed partnerships in the rural areas.

British rule variously replaced indigenous polities or subdued and ruled through them. There was authority superseded (Mughal India, Southern Rhodesia), incorporated (princely states, Gulf sheikhdoms, Buganda, Northern Nigeria, Malaya, Zanzibar), and created (northern Ghana, Iraq, Kenya, Palestine, southern Sudan). The trick was to try and persuade people that the British were not alien invaders but legitimate rulers, governing not just by right of conquest but because they were beneficent successors of previous dynasties (until the 1850s the British were careful to keep the last Moghul empire enthroned, shorn of all power but useful for maintaining the fiction that the British were merely ruling on his behalf). The system of indigenous authority and its historicized political traditions was essential to British rule. At its best, British rule was barely visible; traditional leaders, such as Nigerian emirs or Malayan sultans, did the 'ruling', British 'residents' or 'district officers' providing an invisible hand on the tiller in the background, at least when it came to the level of authority concerning chiefs, princes, and the people. But at higher levels, the British were very much in the driving seat. No indigenous leader, no matter how powerful, would be allowed to treat with a foreign power or to possess military power, and the functions of the central treasury and colony-wide levels of government and administration were exclusively British.

The system of working alongside indigenous junior partners, applied consistently in most parts of the Empire, was captured in the term 'indirect rule', first applied to African colonial administration though representative of the Empire's preference for ruling through indigenous patrons and clients. During their decolonization struggles, nationalists needed to undermine these 'traditional' leaders and argue that new, representative 'modern' politicians—like themselves—were the way forward.

The 'white' dominions

The Empire's main division was a racial one. On one side of the divide was Britain and the self-governing and increasingly autonomous white-ruled settler colonies, known from 1909 as 'dominions'. From the 1926 Balfour Declaration the dominions were deemed constitutionally 'equal' to Britain as members of the

The main classifications within the Empire were:

The empire of settlement (the 'white' dominions)

The Indian empire

The colonial empire

Condominiums (territories ruled jointly with another power)

Treaty-based client states

League of Nations 'mandates' (former German and Ottoman colonies)

The informal empire

British Commonwealth, which became the Commonwealth of Nations in 1946 reflecting the organization's increasingly egalitarian composition as British influence over the dominions declined and decolonization created new nation-states. Almost as soon as they had been founded, the colonies that were to form the larger conglomerations of America, Australia, Canada, New Zealand, and South Africa wanted to be as self-governing as possible, asserting the 'right' of 'free born' Englishmen to rule themselves. Early settlers in places such as Jamaica, St Kitts, and Virginia had done the same, forming their own legislative assemblies that were often at loggerheads with the policies of the British crown and its appointed gubernatorial representatives.

It soon became the aspiration of white settler colonies to achieve 'responsible government' (i.e. internal autonomous parliamentary government based on a bicameral legislature, its decisions subject to the British crown). Not without reservations, London acceded from the mid-nineteenth century onwards, as long as the settler colony in question was considered viable, which in practice meant financially solvent, able to maintain law and order, and not excessively (in London's eyes) cruel to the indigenous population.

London wanted to fulfil settler aspirations to run their own affairs to the greatest extent possible and avoid a repeat of the rebellion that had led the American colonies to leave the Empire and form the United States. Lord Durham's report of 1839 came up with a self-government formula that became a blueprint for dominion autonomy within a British-led imperial system. Though enjoying significant autonomy, these territories remained dependent upon Britain because Britain was responsible for their foreign affairs and defence, purchased the lion's share of their exports, supplied their imports, provided requisite inward investment, and held their sterling balances in London. In all of the colonies of white settlement, the indigenous people were subjugated, usually confined to specially demarcated 'native reserves'. Though never attaining coveted dominion status, Southern Rhodesia was a self-governing colony—which is why its white minority rulers declared unilateral independence from Britain in 1965 when the 'mother country' threatened to force black majority rule upon it - and the white settlers of Kenya unsuccessfully campaigned for this status too.

India and the colonial empire

The rest of the Empire was entirely different from this white-dominated settler state component. It was entirely different in that it was an empire of non-whites ruled by whites. Though indigenous elites—African chiefs, Hashemite kings, Indian princes, and Gulf sheikhs—were part of the ruling team and could wield immense power in relation to their people's daily lives, they were subordinate to the representatives of the British monarch and their provincial and district officers. This was ultimately the case even where the British presence was a light one. Any of these local rulers could be deposed if they strayed from the 'advice' that they were offered or if they rocked the boat or made sheep's eyes at a rival colonial power. The indigenous rulers were disarmed, allowed only (and if they were very senior indeed) to maintain small 'parade ground' military formations designed for ceremonial, not combat, duties. They could jostle for honours, such as the Star of India, specially created extensions of the British state's network of patronage; they could compete for the highest number of gun salutes their station warranted when visiting London for coronations. But they could not compete for political power at the highest level. This was a measure of their and their societies' subordination to colonial rule, a blunt but accurate barometer of where power lay in the imperial system.

So these were the two main 'types' of overseas holding in the British Empire—the white settler states that, though tied to Britain by all sorts of visible and invisible ties, were internally self-governing and increasingly autonomous within the imperial framework; and the rest of the Empire, primarily located in Africa, South Asia, and South-East Asia though with significant islands and enclaves in the Atlantic, the Caribbean, the Far East, the Mediterranean, the Indian Ocean, and the Pacific. The non-white Empire was ruled by British civil servants and their indigenous chiefly or princely collaborators, supported by low-grade indigenous staff and the all-important British-officered indigenous police and armed forces.

There were two main components within this empire of non-whites ruled by whites (or blacks ruled by blues, as one wag had it, reflecting the prevalence of Oxbridge sports 'blues' in the colonial administrative service). There was on the one hand the Indian empire, and on the other hand the colonial empire. India was ruled directly as 'British India' and indirectly through alliance with over 300 princes, each ruling his own fiefdom, supervised from London by the India Office. The Colonial Office was responsible for the scores of other territories that comprised the Empire, mostly crown colonies and protectorates though including treaty-related kingdoms and League of Nations mandates' (see below). The Foreign Office had a cameo role in colonial administration by virtue of its stewardship of the Sudan and other condominiums.

Mandates and condominiums

Run in a similar manner to colonies, but occupying a different category in terms of international law, mandates were former colonies of the German and the Ottoman empires transferred to Britain at the end of the First World War. Thus Britain ruled, 'in trust' on behalf of the League of Nations, (part of) former German Cameroons, Iraq, Nauru, New Guinea, Palestine, South-West Africa, Tanganyika, (part of) former German Togoland, Transjordan, and Western Samoa. Another category of imperial territory in terms of legal status was the condominium, a form of joint rule with another colonial power. Thus Britain ruled the New Hebrides in conjunction with the French, and the Sudan in conjunction with the Egyptians, though in the latter case Britain was by far the senior partner by virtue of the fact that it effectively dominated Egypt too. Briefly at the end of the nineteenth century Britain jointly ruled the Samoan Islands with America and Germany, and more recently, in 2001, the British government suggested offering Spain a condominium—joint sovereignty—over Gibraltar, an idea rejected by the Gibraltarian people.

Treaty relationships and informal empire

There were then the countries which were not formally part of the British Empire but had treaty relations with Britain making Britain responsible for their foreign affairs and their protection. In the Gulf, these included Bahrain, Kuwait, Oman, and Qatar as well as the seven emirates that later formed the United Arab Emirates. From 1900 until 1970 Britain had a Treaty of Friendship with Tonga in the South Pacific too. Finally, there was the 'informal empire', not a classification acknowledged by the British government at any juncture, but a term coined by historians to help conceptualize Britain's relations with a number of non-Empire territories that it nevertheless had considerable influence over. In introducing this concept the renowned imperial historians Jack Gallagher and Ronald Robinson argued that the 'red on the map' formal empire was just the tip of the iceberg when considering Britain's global power and influence. Egypt provides an example: Britain only formally ruled it for eight years (1914–22) but maintained a pivotal strategic base there for nearly eighty, during which time Egypt's sovereignty was severely impaired by Britain's oversight of its foreign relations, its economic position within the country, and its enormous military presence on Egyptian soil. Throughout much of Latin America, in China, and in country's such as Persia, Britain wielded significant influence, as well as in less well-known cases, such as Chile, Thailand, and Tibet. Regimes in these regions often relied on Britain for investment and export and import markets and leaned culturally towards it too, leading to a degree of dependency that granted Britain political leverage and 'spheres of influence' beyond its actual imperial domain. The extent to which this actually translated into power equating to the power Britain wielded in its imperial domains has been contested by historians. Nevertheless, whether Britain acted as a 'big brother' or a bullying master, the concept of informal empire opened up an important new vista in terms of understanding global power relations (and it is sometimes employed by those exploring American power today).

In answering the question 'What was the British Empire?', its physical extent and the political nature of its constituent parts is only part of the story. We now turn to look at some of the other ways in which the Empire can be defined.

Chapter 2
Defining empire: key characteristics

Having defined the Empire in terms of its constituent political and juridical parts, this chapter offers a mosaic of some of the Empire's main defining features beyond its physical presence. Once beyond the 'hard edged' definition of Empire as a geopolitical entity—chunks of territory that were 'red on the map'—answers to the question 'what was the British Empire?' become less clear. This is because defining features, such as its cultural dimensions, are much more amorphous and definitions depended on individual people's experiences, which differed widely. Like any supranational entity (such as today's European Union or United Nations), the British Empire had multifaceted and contested realities, meanings, and projected images: it was in large measure an abstract. As Mark Crinson writes:

> When we try to picture empire we might end up with a group of acts, objects and events—tracts of land, biscuit tins, administrative regimes, ceremonies and processions, military conquests and displacements of peoples—no single one of which can be taken to stand for empire in itself although some might be separated out as the 'hard facts' of colonialism. The reason why it is difficult to capture this heterogeneous assortment of things in an image is because empire is an abstraction, or at least as much of an abstraction as words like 'nation' or 'heritage'; empire might be used as the name of a typewriter or a music hall. But, like 'nation' or

'heritage', empire is an overarching ideological construct; it is a particular way of drawing together a host of disparate things so that their collective meaning is made apparent.

The key characteristics explored in this chapter include the Empire's economic status, its cultural dimensions, its existence as a system of knowledge and as a racial construction, its operation as a strategic alliance, its impact on built environments and the natural world, and the role played by anti-colonial opposition in its definition.

An economic bloc and field of opportunity

The British Empire was a coherent inter-territorial trading zone, meaning that a distinct imperial economy existed and functioned as a bloc in the international economy. As well as being a trading zone, the imperial economy featured flows of capital and investment, primarily from the City of London outwards, and pooled sterling resources as London kept hold of the imperial purse-strings. Dynamic change attended the economic evolution of the Empire as what has been labelled the 'first' British Empire—a mercantile, protectionist system based on commercial regulation and trading commodities such as sugar, tobacco, furs, cotton goods, and spices—was superseded by the 'second' British Empire a free trading, *industrial* empire which oversaw the birth of the classic metropole-periphery links between the factories of industrial Britain and scores of raw material-producing colonies that also served as export markets. This encouraged the development of peripheral economies centred on a British core; colonies produced raw materials (Australian wool, Indian cotton) that British industry could convert into finished goods for export, and they also produced the foodstuffs that fed the increasingly urban and non-agricultural British people. Argentinian beef, Canadian wheat, Australasian lamb and dairy products, South African fruit—all of these items joined the products of the earlier empire, such as sugar and tea, to stock the British larder. African slaves were paid for with trade goods and then used to purchase North American exports, and Indian opium was used to pay for Chinese tea and silks.

The power of the British state and Britain's advanced industrial economy and institutions were the bedrock of imperial expansion and strength during the 'second' empire. The convergence of cheap labour, new transport technologies, plentiful water and coal, and captive imperial markets gave the industries of northern Britain a period of global dominance. Emigration underpinned a new division of labour in the growing international economy, one effect of which was to put new strains on native peoples everywhere, another to make transnationalism—living and identifying with more than one country or place—a normal way of life for many people. Overseas markets grew in importance in the nineteenth century, as did the resources of the Empire. The City of London became the world's financial capital, sterling the main currency of international trade. Britain's balance of payments came to depend on multilateral settlements underpinned by a distinctive pattern of specialization between exporters of manufactures and primary producers. The flow of goods, finance, and migrants was enhanced from the mid-nineteenth century by technological improvements such as railways, steamships, underwater cables, and telegraph lines. Innovations in banking and company organization helped British and multinational companies and institutions operate on a global scale and succeed in capital intensive and highly sophisticated industries such as deep level mining.

The imperial economy fostered rapid growth in tropical production and the Empire also produced key metals, including copper, gold, iron, steel, and tin. The 'imperial treasure trove' contained a host of precious raw materials, including sisal, oil, pyrethrum, oilseeds, pyrites, and sea-island cotton. In 1939 the British Empire produced a significant share of the world's total output of key raw materials: 15.6 per cent of the bauxite; 37.6 per cent of the chrome ore; 24.8 per cent of the coal; 29.8 per cent of the copra; 17 per cent of the cotton; 12.9 per cent of the iron; 98.9 per cent of the jute; 35.9 per cent of the lead ore; 36.1 per cent of the manganese; 87.9 per cent of the nickel ore; 42.5 per cent of the palm oil; 51.9 per cent of the rubber; 39.2 per cent of the tin ore; 25.2 per cent of the tungsten ore; 34.8 per cent of the vanadium ore; 45.7 per cent of the wool; and 29 per cent of the zinc ore. Peasant agriculture, plantations, and mines were the most significant forms of imperial production. Chartered companies, cartels, and multinationals such as Anglo-Persian Oil (later BP), Cadbury, De Beers, HSBC, Tate and Lyle, and Unilever were the offspring of Britain's imperial economy and the consumer culture that it fostered. Infrastructural development in the colonies was heavily influenced by the need to extract resources as well as to provide strategic access, most noticeably in the routes of pioneering colonial road and rail networks.

Western technologies—of harbours, railways, telegraphs, hydrology, mining, and sanitation—went hand in hand with empire and its development as an economic unit, creating nodal points of transport and communication, developing new ports and cities, and opening remote hinterlands to the emerging global economy. Botanical research and cross-pollination transformed the economies of regions such as South-East Asia, as Daniel Headrick writes, whilst barrages and canals increased the agricultural output of Egypt and India and mining linked southern and central Africa to the outside world. Businesses were able to profit because the politics of empire offered them shelter. They could act and innovate in ways that would have been impossible in coherent, independent, non-Western states. Railways were built in India because of guarantees provided by the government; shipping lines flourished because of the government mail subsidies that went with them, as well as government's desire to sponsor the accumulation of vessels that could be requisitioned during times of war; cable companies received exclusive rights and subsidies; and mining companies received concessions and favourable labour laws.

5. Pears' soap advertisement, 1885. One of the most egregious examples of advertising and the association of empire with civilization, and of civilization with whiteness

The British Empire was for many people a field of opportunity—somewhere to escape to, to attempt to make oneself, to invest in, all with a range of privileges and protections by virtue of its being British ruled. James Mill famously characterized it as a 'vast system of outdoor relief for the upper classes', whilst others have emphasized its role as a field of sexual opportunity or pleasurable pursuits such as safari. For anthropologists, archaeologists, scientists, and a host of other specialists, the Empire provided a vast laboratory in which they could experiment and enjoy rights of privileged access. The British Empire provided a field of opportunity for other Western and sometimes (when it suited British interests) non-Western actors too, such as the Tata iron and steel family, encouraged when import substitution in India became beneficial to the Empire. It was remarkably multinational; German Lutherans established themselves in South Australia; Scandinavians flocked to the American colonies; American missionaries prospered in British-created enclaves in China; and many Americans, Austrians, and Germans benefited from the Empire's investment in security and infrastructure and were able to operate within its bounds and make money from it. Its major entrepôt settlements, such as Hong Kong, Penang, and Singapore, were melting pots that nurtured the business endeavours of a multiracial entrepreneurial class. They also acted as safe havens for people fleeing oppressive regimes; Penang's population was swelled by Malays escaping Siamese attacks in Kedah, Eurasians fleeing religious persecution in Siam, Chinese moving away from Manchu oppression, and South Indians seeking a better life.

As a realm of business activity the Empire was cosmopolitan. Whilst (for instance) elements of the German press might lambast Britain for its bullying policies towards the Boers, some Germans applauded Britain's resolute action to assert order in South Africa by defeating the Boers in the Anglo-Boer War (1899-1902) and facilitating the unfettered operations of the Randlords, the mixed nationality entrepreneurs who controlled the South African diamond and gold industries. Similarly, the political bounds that delimited the empires of other European powers were no barrier to the activities of British capital and economic forces: the British South Africa Company, for instance, was heavily involved in Portuguese East Africa and German South-West Africa. In an earlier period, war with Spain secured Britain the right to sell slaves in the coveted Spanish American market, and British economic vigour led to the commercial penetration of the ailing Spanish Empire.

A cultural universe

The British Empire was a cultural interface, its colonial structures forming the juncture between expanding Western culture in all its forms and an array of different indigenous cultures. The differences were immense, the impact of colonial culture varied, though usually, in one way or another, profound. As the tentacles of imperial expansion and culture bored their way into local societies and cultures, imperialism became both a disruptive and creative force. Those who provided the Empire's 'public' face, such as colonial administrators, traders, or missionaries, could affect even the most intimate realms of peoples' lives. Colonialism oversaw the penetration of Western material culture across the globe, a phenomenon of which it was both a product and a propagator. The colonial state brought bureaucracies, legal systems, modes of land tenure and marriage, educational institutions, spiritual ideas, and a degree of cultural diffusion which made its impact on everyday life deeper and more enduring than that achieved by most other empires. It significantly reshaped institutions or developed entirely new ones. It brought capitalism, with its attendant opportunities and threats, winners and losers. Whether one chose to spurn it or not, colonialism heralded economic and political changes that were bound to impact upon culture. It proclaimed an allegedly superior culture, alluringly associated with power and success. Nelson Mandela offered an insight into the meaning of being ruled by aliens: 'The education I received was a British education, in which British ideas, British culture, and British institutions were automatically assumed to be superior. There was no such thing as African culture.'

Whilst the Empire was not a cultural juggernaut, and people in remote regions and those furthest away from settlers and urban centres might have had their lives impinged upon only erratically and indirectly, colonial rule had deep structural implications. This was partly the result of the opening of societies to Western consumer culture, to the cash economy, to aspirational lifestyles, and to new ideas of leisure and of labour. It was also born of the desire of some people to associate themselves with the culture of the ruling elite, to learn its language, to adopt its modes of dress and comportment, its marital practices and visions of domesticity, to transform themselves and perhaps their societies in beneficial ways. There were then the activities of missionaries, who deliberately set out to change the way people thought, worshipped, dressed, farmed, and lived. But the forces of imperialism did not simply breeze into distant parts of the world and reshape local identities, and empire was not alone as an engine of cultural change. New kinds of consumer habits fostered by the expansion of trade and communications were global phenomena – in Europe, as well as the non-European world – as were new forms of knowledge, both secular and spiritual.

Whilst the Empire oversaw cultural diffusion, one of its leitmotifs from the nineteenth century was a separation between European culture and that of non-Europeans. The Empire was always contradictory on this front; it wanted people to be more 'like us', but on the other hand did not want them to become *too* like us, lest this destroy their 'traditional' culture (which the British wanted to preserve) and implant the kinds of socio-economic changes that the Industrial Revolution had brought to Britain, and that many colonial administrators deplored. It was contradictory also because at the heart of imperialism lay a fundamental divide; rulers cannot allow the ruled to become *too* like them, because this would denote equality, and empires are not made up of equals. In the nineteenth century, a significant debate took place in Britain about whether the enormous population of the new Indian empire should be Anglicized or allowed to develop along its own separate lines. Thomas Macaulay, in his famous 'Minute on Education' of 1835, urged the creation of 'a class of person, Indian in blood and colour, but English in taste, in opinions, in morals, and in intellect'—a class of 'brown Englishmen'. The cost of attempting to become more European could be high; becoming a Christian, it was said, meant ceasing to be an African because of the cultural changes it demanded, and there was always the chance that in the attempt a person would become a maroon, shunned by his own community whilst not accepted by the European one.

The problems with attempts to change other people were numerous: on the one hand, it was by no means an agreed-upon policy (colonial officials, for instance, rarely shared the missionaries' enthusiasm for cultural change and would much rather leave indigenous people to their own gods, marital practices, and beliefs and concentrate solely on keeping people acquiescent and paying their taxes). Also, it was very unevenly applied, because it was left largely to private enterprise (mainly missionaries), which had finite resources. It also faltered on people's resistance and indifference, and one of imperialism's greatest unresolved contradictions: even those who became Europeanized were not welcomed into the fold. Educational institutions, particularly the missionary schools, public schools, and universities that the Empire created, symbolized these contradictions. Their aim to give people a British-style education was circumscribed by the fact that it could lead to demands for equality and independence, and so the education they offered needed to be controlled. The imperial enterprise could not allow education to nurture political discourse—because that always led, in the first instance, to demands for a greater share of imperial authority and then, when this was withheld, to demands for independence from British rule. These educational institutions also ignored extant systems of indigenous knowledge and education. As Eric Ashby said, British education in India excluded 'the whole of oriental learning and religion' and purveyed to Hindus and Muslims 'a history and philosophy whose roots lie exclusively in the Mediterranean and in Christianity'. It communicated 'the examinable skeleton of European civilization without ensuring that the values and standards which give flesh to these bones are communicated too'.

Wherever they went, the British became self-appointed experts on people's cultures. They knew best, they always claimed, how to record them, to codify them, restore them, and preserve them. They attacked indigenous practices (such as polygamy, bridewealth, and circumcision) without understanding their social function. In India they became transfixed by caste, and their imagination of it shaped the way they dealt with social structures and actually magnified its significance. In Africa, they believed that people lived in 'tribes', and so created them where they had not previously existed. Where something of that nature *did* already exist, they attempted to make them conform to their own codified version, helping concretize tribal identities and divisions where previously they had been more fluid mechanisms of organization and identity. It was an ironic measure of the power of empire that the British became the expert interpreters of other peoples' cultures—even to those people themselves. Jomo Kenyatta pilloried the '"professional friends of the African" who are prepared to maintain their friendship for eternity as a sacred duty, provided only that the African will continue to play the part of an ignorant savage so that they can monopolize the office of interpreting his mind and speaking for him'.

Europeans were bursting with prescriptions about how others should live, enamoured with 'traditional' society as a subconscious way of 'preserving' cultures and protecting them from the horrors of modernity, one of the great imperial paradoxes - preaching progress without change and upholding 'superior' European methods but discouraging indigenous peoples from ever becoming European or modern.

Recruiting for the British Army in the remote Okavango Delta in 1941, the Resident Commissioner of the Bechuanaland

Protectorate, Lieutenant-Colonel Aubrey Forsyth Thompson, reported that the people 'don't know what government is or why anyone is fighting at all'. Yet even though the Batawana people of Ngamiland clearly had limited contact with the protectorate's skeletal colonial administration, limited knowledge of its function or its relevance, and only a rudimentary conception of world events, they were nonetheless deeply affected by their colonial status. The taxes that their chiefs collected were imposed by the colonial government in far-off Mafeking, and often required contractual labour in South Africa's mineral mines in order to pay them; the cash economy, together with its new consumer goods, was a product of capitalist globalization; the 'native law and custom' that their British-created tribunals administered had been codified by a British anthropologist; and, working through their chiefs, the army recruiters obtained the manpower they needed to support imperial armies fighting Rommel in the Western Desert. Furthermore, by virtue of their subjection to an apparently distant empire and the connections to phenomena such as the international economy and world war that it forged, the availability and the price of the very food that they ate were set for them.

Imperialism and the colonial state introduced novel notions of territorial boundaries and demanded a fundamental re-imagining of space and human relationships. It critiqued, challenged, and in significant ways changed people's cultures. It introduced literacy and new concepts of medicine, spirituality, and property ownership. Imperialism imposed Western concepts and rituals of time upon indigenous populations, extending to them the dubious benefits of the twenty-four-hour clock and the Gregorian calendar. It defined their racial and ethnic categories, in ways that mattered and could seldom be ignored—if you were from one particular 'tribe', for example, you might be denied access to certain types of employment; if you were from one particular 'reserve', you might be denied access to other parts of a colony without official documentation. British rule shaped gender roles too, and propagated new concepts, such as domesticity and the benefit of lighter complexions, spawning a range of skin-lightening products that remain popular to this day. Imperialisms' impact on identity could be striking; it firmed up ethnic boundaries, it imagined and created 'martial races', and sharpened the divide between Hindus and Muslims. Indigenous people were energetic participants in the innumerable projects of identity construction and transformation, seeking to benefit where they could, though working within British-defined parameters. It was a measure of power that, even when the British misunderstood what was going on, their faulty prognoses formed the basis of subsequent developments.

Empire and British culture

Things flowed both ways, and British culture and identity were influenced by empire and general engagement with the wider world, from immigrants and loan words in the English language to diet, consumer goods, buildings (such as the bungalow), furniture, décor, and a range of cultural representations in literature, advertising, music, and the arts. British popular culture contained many references to the Empire and the non-European world and many British institutions had distinctly imperial dimensions, such as the monarchy, the military, and the church, clubs, societies, and schools, innumerable associations and leagues, missionary societies, museums, theatres, and businesses. Through them all, knowledge of the non-European world was gathered and then presented to the British public.

In terms of the Empire's impact on British culture, there has been great debate in recent years. Some historians have claimed that British culture was 'steeped' or 'saturated' in imperialism, the very concept of British nationality dependent upon it. Empire is said to have played an integral part in metropolitan values, thoughts, ideas, and practices. Catherine Hall argues that empire was part of everyday life for Britons between the late eighteenth century and the end of the Second World War, John MacKenzie that empire

6. Aboriginal dancers perform for Queen Elizabeth II during her visit to Clontarf Aboriginal college in Perth, Australia, 2011. The Queen's sixteenth official visit to Australia—she first visited on the Empire Tour that followed her coronation—it was timed to coincide with the Commonwealth Heads of Government Meeting. The association of the monarchy with the Empire was cemented by Victoria and her son Edward VII, and his son George V. The monarchy and the Commonwealth are among the most visible legacies of empire

constituted a vital aspect of national identity and race consciousness, even if complicated by regional, rural, urban, and class contexts. Others, notably Bernard Porter, claim that it was much less significant, and that proponents of the opposite view risk overcompensating for the previous neglect of the subject of empire's impact upon Britain by seeing empire in everything. Empire, this side of the debate claims, was irrelevant for most Britons most of the time. However much they may have been surrounded by evidence of empire, 'ordinary' British people, they argue, were unlikely to interrogate it, or connect it all up. Ronald Hyam claims that his generation was much more concerned about dodging German rockets and avoiding nuclear destruction than about the Empire, and writes that if someone had mentioned the Empire when he was a schoolboy, he would have assumed they meant the Chiswick Empire, a nearby cinema.

Whilst it is necessary to be cautious when considering what people in the past thought, about Britain's place in the world, about empire, about non-Europeans, this should not prevent careful assessment. Like other turf wars within the field of imperial history, protagonists on both sides sometimes talk past each other, and historical cockfighting can obscure common ground. Surely it is not too much to say that during the days of empire many British people looked down upon non-British people. Others, who may have had no particular opinion, acquiesced in the formulation of a puissant world view based upon superiority and right to a sufficient extent that it did not hinder the operation of imperial rule. Few British people would have considered an African 'tribesman' an equal; perhaps an equal before God, but not as 'developed' and probably in need of the uplift that British rule purported to bestow.

A wide constituency saw Britain's fate as tied up with its overseas interests and assumed the unchallengeable right of British migrants abroad to seize the lands of indigenous people. 'It can hardly be doubted that the sense of being part of a larger political world extending far beyond Britain was very widely diffused… [E]ntrenched vested interests, often commanding a loud public voice, could play upon this awareness of a "greater" Britain on whose power and prestige "little" England depended. But they could not assume a broad public sympathy for all types of empire and on every occasion. Nor of course did the "imperial interest" speak with one voice or express a single concern'.

British culture was significantly influenced by imperialism and the perspectives on the non-European world that it bred. This holds true even as one agrees with the sceptics that the majority of the public were ignorant about the specifics of empire and that, beyond certain upper classes and groups of people with empire-related lives, most

NO. 50

7. **Australia in London, advertisement for cure-all 'bile beans'. c. 1900 and an example of representations of the wider world in British culture.**

people were disinterested in it. The important point is that *because of*, not despite, this general lack of interest or commitment, empire could exist and expand. All it required was a general level of acceptance—and this meant something much more fundamental than specific knowledge of empire or interest in it. It meant an imperial world view, one that acquiesced in colonization and possession of empire, seeing nothing remarkable in it, and possibly good things associated with it. This world view was founded on widely held if inchoate assumptions about European, and particularly British, superiority, of the alien-ness and frequently the backwardness of non-Europeans who, in turn, needed to be aided by those more civilized, or at least set to one side so that their resources could be exploited for the benefit of mankind. Increasingly, this was a world view predicated upon racial hierarchies. If these ideas were less practically significant in Britain itself, they were hugely significant in the large portions of the earth under the sway of British settlers. The burgeoning settler states were premised on the decline, subjugation, and dispossession of their indigenous inhabitants. Not to compute that as a fundamental aspect of an imperial culture is to lose sight of the wood for the trees.

A system of knowledge

Tony Ballantyne argues that empire 'was not simply about extending informal political influence, establishing economic domination, or securing sovereignty, but it was a much broader set of asymmetrical relationships grounded in the desire of the colonizer to exert mastery over the colonized society, its natural and human resources, and its cultural forms. As a part of this, imperialists frequently appropriated indigenous knowledge as they generated "colonial knowledge", produced out of and enabling resource exploitation, commerce, conquest, and colonization.' The authority of colonial states rested on their ability to collate and distil knowledge of local terrains and cultures in maps, ethnographies, grammars, botanical drawings, legal codes, encyclopedias, research centres, specimens, and censuses. Through these processes, for example, Indian words, artefacts, and identities 'were wrenched out of their indigenous context and fashioned into new bodies of knowledge that served the needs of the British, but often bore little relation to indigenous reality'. Empires were important vectors for the development and spread of Western science and other forms of specialist endeavour. Cartography was important in surveying for military campaigns, tax assessment, and the projection of the idea of India as a unified political unit. Medicine, despite claims of scientific neutrality, was embedded in imperial structures of domination, and communications technology was crucial to the power of the colonial state.

A racial construction

The British Empire was a racial construct in which whites were of higher status than non-whites. Wherever one travelled in the Empire, the white person was the sahib, tuan, baas, bwana, or master—whatever his station and whatever he might have been called behind his back. The British were often distant and arrogant, especially once Victorian decorum and morals, and Britain's growing power, confidence, and sense of mission, had opened a chasm between Britons and 'natives', eradicating earlier habits that were often more relaxed, respectful, and intermingled. The British were exceedingly proprietorial—it was 'their' Empire, their playground, and they were the ruling race even if only a minor functionary in a department store or a private soldier. The stentorian cry of 'Boy! Whisky-soda!' echoed in all the Empire's clubs. The British behaved, for example, as if they owned Kenya, which to all intents and purposes they did once they had purloined the 'White' Highlands and other choice tracts of land; they walked supreme through the streets of Cairo and took the Pyramids as their own special place in which to picnic and frolic. They could emigrate if things went bad at home or they needed an escape or just an adventure. The sense of British proprietorship leaps off the pages of contemporary memoirs and novels. In the colonial world, the British were monarchs of all they surveyed; and it was their impregnable air of entitlement that so vexed and goaded indigenous people, especially those who were themselves diminished or emasculated leaders of society as a result of British rule. Across the globe imperialism constructed 'the native', and whether he was a 'child-like' or 'lascivious' African, an 'inscrutable' Chinese man, or an 'effeminate' Bengali, he was the living opposite of the white man. 'The natives' were simply part of the scenery, the very term itself denoting a stolid backwardness inviting Western improvement and dynamism, as well as attachment to the soil that the aliens now sought to control. Even for those who did not share this view, even for those who purported wholeheartedly to love and admire other cultures, it was very common to adopt the position, often unthinkingly, that they needed European help, reform, restitution, or civilization. This was a prevalent way of viewing the world at the time, common in all Western societies. British people out in the colonies lived with themselves as colonialists because of their deep and abiding sense of *paternalism*, the belief that they were genuinely helping people who needed it.

Non-whites *could* achieve some social and economic advancement, and those of high birth usually constituted an elite, partnering the British as junior participants in the business of rule, administration, and economic activity. But even members of the elite, even the ultra-rich who had schooled at Eton, might be denied membership of the highest-ranking clubs, or might be barred on 'Europeans only' days. And even they, whilst co-opted and woven into the fabric of the imperial great chain of being through honours and gun salutes and coronations or Empire Day parades, were still kept at arm's length, no matter how 'loyal' they were (a key imperial litmus test). Walking across the grounds of the exclusive Gezira Sporting Club in Cairo, the young Edward Said had what he termed an 'explicit colonial encounter'. He ran into the Club Secretary, an Englishman called Mr Pilley, who believed he was trespassing. 'Don't answer back, boy', said the brown-suited, pith-helmeted Mr Pilley, after Said had tried to explain that his father was a club member. 'Just get out, and do it quickly. Arabs aren't allowed here, and you're an Arab!' 'If I hadn't thought of myself as an Arab before', Said wrote, 'I now directly grasped the significance of the designation as truly disabling.'

Whilst hierarchy and class were significant prisms through which colonial peoples were perceived and ranked, race was key. As the nineteenth century developed, pseudo-scientific 'proof' of non-European inferiority became influential, fusing with a common assumption of Anglo-Saxon superiority. There was a new emphasis on race as an explanation and justification of inequality and difference. Attitudes changed quickly. In the space of three decades, for instance, the humanitarian, paternalist assumptions that had influenced the decision to colonize New Zealand had given way to ideas about the inevitability of Maori defeat at the hands of the racially superior settlers. This pattern can be traced in the fate of the Treaty of Waitangi: conceived in 1840 as an instrument to curtail the excesses of the invaders, by 1877 it had been declared a 'simple nullity' by New Zealand Chief Justice James Prendergast, having been signed 'between a civilized nation and a group of savages'.

A strategic and military system

The British Empire was a strategic and military system. What became known as 'imperial defence' (there was a Cabinet Committee of Imperial Defence from the early twentieth century) was founded for most of the Empire's lifespan upon the global power of the Royal Navy, based on dominance in home waters to secure Britain against invasion and a large overseas base infrastructure including control of the world's key waterways and maritime choke points (the Suez Canal, the western entrance to the Mediterranean, the Cape of Good Hope, the Straits of Malacca). Alongside the navy, army garrisons were responsible for the security of colonial borders and 'internal security', which meant suppressing rebellions and 'illicit' political movements. The garrisons provided defensive capabilities for important bases, and a 'firefighting' capability for deployment should trouble break out in a particular region. They were supplied by a British Army rarely more than 200,000 strong in peacetime, though supplemented by a unique asset, the Indian Army, and a gallimaufry of colonial forces such as the Transjordan Frontier Force, the South Persia Rifles, the New South Wales Corps, the Northern Rhodesia Regiment, the Fiji Volunteer Force, and the Hong Kong and

Singapore Garrison Artillery. These land forces were vital, because the expansion of empire and the suppression of innumerable uprisings meant that throughout its history 'savage wars' or 'pacification' campaigns, to use the loaded language of the time, were always ongoing. In the twentieth century, these forces were joined by air force squadrons pre-positioned to defend the Empire against external aggression and, as a 'swift agent of government', to share the burdens of colonial policing with the army and navy. During the world wars of the eighteenth, nineteenth, and twentieth centuries, colonial manpower resources were hugely important, as were the Empire's fleets and squadrons in the major oceans.

Whilst resting on its armed forces and in particular British mastery at sea, the Empire's security also rested on alliances with other great powers, most notably Japan (from 1902 until the 1920s), France (from 1904 until the collapse of France in 1940), and on America in the post-Second World War years. There were always major tensions afflicting imperial defence. Did the possession of overseas outposts make Britain stronger, or merely present it with innumerable defensive nightmares? Such concerns were epitomized by the agonizing over the construction of a new naval base at Singapore, and the eventual failure of the 'Singapore strategy' to defend the eastern empire because, when it needed a strong fleet, Britain's naval resources were tied up defending Britain itself. The tension between an imperial strategy and a continental one informed Britain's defence policy deep into the post-war period. British governments until the 1950s equated the maintenance and defence of empire as crucial to Britain's status as a world power. Others argued that the need to maintain large defence forces, meanwhile, damaged the British economy.

The British Empire was founded, ultimately, on force. Though there was never force available everywhere, and collaborative relationships and the skill of district officials were the day-to-day backbone of the system, *force was certainly present*, even if it was latent. Those who rebelled against the authority of the British Empire tended to find this out the hard way. A gunboat might be dispatched, a company, battalion, brigade or even a division might be sent against them, depending on the scale of the 'unrest' (a common colonial catch-all euphemism) and the prowess of the insurgents, malcontents, rebels, recalcitrants, or terrorists (to plunder the colonial lexicon of terms used to delegitimize opponents). Rebellions were ruthlessly crushed, from the Indian Mutiny to the Mau Mau Emergency. Enemy states and peoples were defeated, from Tippoo Tib to the Mahdi, the Emperor of Burma, and the Boer republics. Uncooperative chiefs, princes, kings, and prime ministers were deposed (and often exiled, usually to remote islands), a lengthy list that came to include the Zulu king Cetshwayo, the Shah of Persia Reza Pahlavi, Egypt's Arabi Pasha, Tshekedi Khama of the Bangwato, the last Moghul emperor Bahadur Shah II, Archbishop Makarios of Cyprus, the Iraqi prime minister Rashid Ali, and the Kandyan king Sri Vikrama Rajasinha. As a related index of imperial power, Britain successfully *disarmed* local polities, and gathered to itself a monopoly of lethal force.

The Empire demonstrated its power to move people and command them most vigorously during times of war, when Whitehall's leash was tightened and every colonial territory, no matter how remote or inhospitable, did as it was bid and provided manpower and material for the war effort. The utilization of imperial resources between 1939 and 1945, for example, represented an astonishing display of imperial power and demonstrated Britain's capacity to conscript and to command. The point is that although the 'dread of our power' was always in part illusory, it was *never* wholly so.

A transformer of the natural world and the built environment

The Empire's globality linked disparate lands, peoples, and species in an unprecedented manner. The growth of the British

Empire created entirely new cities, states, and federations and led to a profound transformation of the natural world.

Empire oversaw an astonishing global transplantation and cross-fertilization as flora, fauna, and microbes were promiscuously moved from one region to another, not always intentionally. Native species were decimated as 'English' trees, shrubs, birds, fish, rodents, and livestock were introduced. 'Useless' plants were exterminated so that productive ones, such as eucalyptus, could be planted. The expansion of cattle- and sheep-farming in Australia and South Africa introduced colonial administrators to the problems of exploitation and control. Like other migrant peoples, wherever the British went their cash crops, food crops, and livestock went with them. The development of plantations, national parks, farmlands, and pasturelands across the world was the direct result of European settlement and its commercial, agricultural, 'sporting', and conservation activities. Whilst shooting the game out of vast tracts of southern Africa, their imported rabbits wreaked havoc among Australia's grasslands, and their tea and rubber plantations transformed landscapes in Asia and South-East Asia. The development of botanical gardens around the world marked the search for lucrative crops and valuable plants, as well as the desire to collect and classify all living things, to identify and to tame the 'exotic', to rationalize the seemingly irrational.

Agricultural activities, extensive plant and animal transfers, forestry, irrigation, and flood control were areas of extensive endeavour in the British Empire. There was a constant tension between the desire to conserve—the Empire can claim some of the most important pioneering work in terms of environmental conservation—and the desire to produce and to profit. A growing body of men of science, through their researches in colonial settings, especially botanical gardens, began to warn of the fragility and exhaustibility of the natural world, though few were prepared to heed them. Others experienced a Pauline conversion, such as Colonel R. W. Burton, a leading exponent of shikar (tiger

8. The colonial built environment: The Sultan Abdul Samad Building, Merdeka Square, Kuala Lumpur. Constructed as the administrative centre of the state of Selangor and named after its then Sultan, the clock tower ('Big Ben') first chimed to coincide with the celebration of Queen Victoria's diamond jubilee in 1897. It frames the padang of Merdeka Square along with other colonial era buildings, including the Royal Selangor Club and St Mary's Cathedral. Redolent of the days of empire, this space has become central to Malaysia's national identity, as it was here that the Union Flag was lowered in 1957

hunting) before realizing how much the tiger population had dwindled and becoming instead a leading conservationist. Such people sought to turn the Empire from plunder to preservation, sometimes invoking wonky science in the process. Frequently the British discovered, 'scientifically', that indigenous habits and practices endangered environments, so set about separating them. Thus, for example, in the Nilgiri Hills the alleged predations of the indigenous population were stopped so that forests could be scientifically improved, resulting in increased timber felling for the market and increased tax revenue for the colonial state. Environmentally, the British were adept at finding out what was 'wrong' with indigenous practices, whilst failing to find any fault in their own.

As well as transforming the natural world, the British Empire oversaw, in a relatively short space of time, astonishing additions to the world's built environment. The layout and zoning of scores of cities and ports around the world is entirely imperial. They mark the international landscape to this day, but might very well, when one thinks about it, not have existed at all. The baronial mansion set down in the African bush or the genesis of 'Western' society in distant Australia epitomize this strangeness, as did the utter bizarreness of English towns cropping up in the foothills of the Himalayas: Chinese merchants from Yarkand, who had travelled over the snow covered ranges to Simla in 1847, were astonished at the sight of a substantial British settlement where logically there should only have been a small Indian village. One can imagine their disorientation. The equivalent, if the imperial boot had ever been on the other foot, would have been thatched rondavels in Wiltshire, or a pagoda rearing its eaves on the Thames embankment. It was madness, really, the sheer incongruity of it all. Tasmania, an island on the other side of the world, had its indigenous population eradicated and replaced by British settlers who soon divided their new homeland into English parishes (Wessex, Essex, Monmouthshire) containing towns and villages named after their British progenitors (Devonport, Launceston, Swansea). What is more, the incongruity does not diminish with time, because the processes of colonization affected such fundamental transformations. Thus to this day Tasmania feels like an English county (Cornwall's long-lost neighbour say). It is firmly part of the 'Western' world despite its extremely 'eastern' location, and its native inhabitants will never come back.

A constantly contested realm

The British Empire was always defined by opposition and the fissiparousness common to all empires and the struggles between nationalism and imperialism that they incubate. From its earliest foundations, fledgling communities of white settlers argued with royally appointed governors about the degree of 'freedom' from

London's control they had a right to enjoy, some defining themselves in opposition to Britain and the British government. If imperial subjects of *British* birth could bridle at imperial control, it is no surprise that those not of British origin, especially when brought forcibly within the Empire's bounds, were apt to contest imperial authority too. Rebellions were frequent, some of the most notable ones mounted by the Empire's white subjects, such as Afrikaners, French Canadians, Irish, and Rhodesians, as well as Egyptians, Indians, Jamaicans, Kikuyu, Iraqis, Malayan Chinese, and Sudanese.

Be it nineteenth-century commentators exercised by the moral dilemmas attached to the sudden acquisition of vast numbers of Indian subjects (would it breed autocratic habits at home?), missionaries bemoaning the evil effects of the opium trade or drawing attention to the 'red rubber' scandal in the Congo, or nationalist critics and activists such as Gandhi, empire was always contested and its manifestations critiqued. The public perception of empire was heavily influenced by the activities of such people, and by the Empire's major reverses, all associated with resistance to British rule, such as the American Revolution, the Indian Mutiny, the Morant Bay mutiny in Jamaica, heavy defeats in Afghanistan and Zululand, the two Boer wars, the Easter Rising in Ireland, risings in Egypt, India, and Iraq at the end of the First World War, and the insurgencies of the 1950s. Colonial administrations and settlers in certain parts of the Empire suffered from a 'rising psychosis', fearing rebellion and always striving to detect the first signs, a measure of the alienness of their rule and their distance from the indigenous people.

The twentieth century became famous for the actions of nationalists and their diverse political parties and movements, from the Jewish Agency to the Muslim League and the Rhodesia Front. They trip off the tongue in a veritable alphabet soup of acronyms: ANC, BDP, INC, IRA, KANU, MCP, TANU, ZANU, ZAPU. Their colourful leaders often became household names,

9. Nationalism and political protest, key solvents of empire: Protesters supporting Zimbabwean independence demonstrate against the Conservative government's handling of the Rhodesia talks, November 1979, Trafalgar Square, London

men such as Gerry Adams, Aung San, Banda, Gandhi, Jinnah, Kenyatta, Makarios, Mandela, Mintoff, Mugabe, Nasser, Nehru, Nkomo, and Nkrumah. Some of the most powerful condemnations of empire came from former colonial officials such as George Orwell and Leonard Woolf, who thought it absurd for one civilization to try to impose its rule upon an entirely different one. Throughout its history the British Empire's character was heavily marked by the activities of opponents and critics, including left-wing intellectuals and proponents of the United Nations idea or the cause of racial equality. As British society became more democratic and liberal and as international society became more egalitarian and international law came to favour the principle of self-determination, ruling an empire became less and less sustainable.

Chapter 3
Engines of expansion

This chapter explores the major impulses that led people to venture overseas and engage in activities that led to imperial expansion. The motive forces included migration, trade, strategic rivalry, and warfare. The trite but truthful answer to the question 'why do empires grow' is 'because they can'. Following from this, the answer to the question 'why did people act in ways that led to empire?' is 'because they could'. George Mallory's answer when asked why he wanted to climb Everest was 'because it's there', and many British people felt the same about the world and the opportunities it offered. European people had the capacity to get overseas and to do things when they arrived—trade, explore, preach, settle—and so they did. There were serious risks, but enough people considered them acceptable, especially as technology and science combined to increase their chances of surviving sea voyages, disease, and hostile indigenes and hostile environments. Others were simply desperate enough – for survival or for glory – to try. There was a world out there to be acted upon, fortunes to be won, lands to be conquered, curiosity to be slaked, souls to be saved. Increasingly, as hazards of climate, distance, and resistance were mastered, it became a British world, and to be a Briton abroad within the Empire's bounds became an exulted status.

Unless the British government, or some other agency, had closed all the ports and immobilized all the ocean-going vessels, there was really no way of stopping people leaving the country and doing things that, as often as not, led to colonization.

A nineteenth-century cartoon captured the unbridled zest for colonialism by depicting a would-be colonist with a ladder staring wistfully at the moon. The existence of the British Empire rested on sufficient tools and motives and indigenous weakness in the face of advancing colonial frontiers. Technological advances fed the growing disparity between Western imperialists and the indigenous societies that they encountered. This, coupled with a permissive intellectual and political environment both internationally and at home, made empire hard to avoid. Empire rested upon a relative absence of rivals capable of threatening Britain's position in Europe, and rivals overseas who could be beaten or accommodated; on American isolationism; and on the acquiescence, or ineffectual resistance, of vast swathes of the non-European world.

Relative power vis-à-vis indigenous societies and great power rivals

The expansion and contraction of the British Empire reflected Britain's power relative to indigenous polities, and that of other 'great power' states. One of the most important causes of expansion was technological and scientific advance. As Tony Hopkins reminds us, control over the means of destruction combined with a sharp reduction in the costs of coercion caused by technological progress enabled vast extensions to the Empire. Advances were not confined to the hardware of technology, such as guns, railways, steamships, cable and wireless telegraphy, and deep-level mining machinery; it also encompassed organizational technology such as bureaucratic structures, innovations such as the infantry square and the management of complex lines of communication, joint stock companies, banks, and revenue-gathering census information. Scientific and technological advances were handmaidens of empire, simultaneously reinforcing and demonstrating British superiority and calling forth greater colonial endeavour. The British Empire oversaw a profusion of scientific initiatives and circuits, including networks of agronomists, anatomists, botanists, foresters, geologists, marine biologists, oceanographers, and physicists.

The Empire grew when the international setting was permissive—when power disparities between the West and the Rest were buttressed by a range of intellectual, psychological, and political factors that made empire more likely to occur and to be tolerated or actively welcomed. Until the nineteenth century it was considered acceptable to conquer overseas territory and subjugate foreign people, to enslave them or exploit them as cheap labour; to convert or 'uplift' them, allegedly for their own good, or to take the natural resources which occurred in their lands, justified by the claim that if the natives were incapable of utilizing God-given resources, it was the duty of a superior civilization to do so instead. At home, whilst never unopposed, this was not generally deemed reprehensible; amongst Britain's great power peers it was considered normal, indeed even dutiful and admirable. To be an empire builder was to be an adventurer, a hero, a doer of deeds in a world that needed to be taken in hand. There were as yet no international bodies, such as the United Nations or human rights charities, to effectively oppose it, and the voices of empire's critics and its nationalist opponents were at this stage too weak to be of much consequence. Furthermore, the rights of indigenous people were barely considered, the defeat of their resistances to European encroachment viewed largely as inconsequential, their lives of little value. Internal opposition to colonial forces and imperial rule was delegitimized in a host of ways, and crushed with relative ease if it were not accommodated.

When coupled with the evident capacity of the agents of British expansion to enter distant lands and establish the trade links or settlements that they desired, this all meant that the price of colonization was relatively *cheap*. It did not cost vast amounts in terms of the nation's blood and treasure; maintaining it did not degrade Britain's economic and military resources; and it did not seriously diminish its political and moral capital or its international reputation. Indeed, other nations envied Britain its empire, and Britons could even preach of the need to 'take up the white man's burden', Rudyard Kipling's exhortation to America when it defeated Spain and occupied its colonies. This very clearly established colonization as a *duty* of civilized powers, a notion at the heart of the powerful civilizing mission element in nineteenth-century imperialism—part genuinely held belief, part self-justificatory foundation myth of empire. Augmenting this was the equally prevalent argument that without the blessing of British rule, indigenous societies would fall apart.

Liberals did not oppose the existence of empire or even its expansion, 'as long as it could be represented as a system uncorrupting at home and contributing to world peace and improvement'. The apparently oxymoronic (from today's viewpoint) motto 'empire and liberty' was common at the high noon of empire before the First World War. There was a genuine belief that administrators, missionaries, and others at the colonial coalface were 'lighting the dark places', supervising 'great works, roads, railways, telegraphs, wharfs', and directing Africans and Asians through a 'wise and benevolent guardianship'. Paternalism, and the belief in doing good things, was a central part of the imperial mission, becoming stronger as liberal tendencies became more embedded in Britain itself.

The other key reason why the British Empire grew is that indigenous societies were unable to successfully resist colonial intrusions. In many cases, colonial rule crept gradually across an unsuspecting region; at one moment the Maasai, for instance, were allied with the newly arrived British, raiding their enemies and taking their cattle in tandem with a British drive to bring 'unfriendly' tribes to heel; the next, the Maasai were being moved off their land and their nomadic way of life was under threat, the British now strong enough in the nascent 'East Africa

Protectorate' to dispense with their assistance. At first, local leaders rarely perceived the enormity of what was taking place, and might ally with Europeans in order to pursue their own goals, unaware of the magnitude of the threat to their independence posed by the odd European trader, concession-hunter, missionary, or explorer. They only tended to find out that they were the thin end of a very big wedge when it was far too late to effectively coordinate local resistance. It was often at this point of realization, maybe a few years after the British had first arrived, that serious rebellions began, and were ruthlessly crushed. The great pity for indigenous societies was that, like the Maori, they could not predict the tidal wave of settlement that was to follow the initial arrival of a handful of Europeans, and act in an appropriate, unified manner.

The law of unintended consequences

Another important cause of imperial expansion was what might be termed the law of unintended consequences. This embraces the idea that many actions and contacts that led to the creation of colonial situations did not have imperial expansion as their intention. The law of unintended consequences governed much of the British Empire's expansion. Wherever the British fetched up, sooner or later traders, missionaries, explorers, settlers, or military officers would blunder into a situation that led to imperial expansion; Britain was a bull that brought its own china shop. The Empire expanded in a piecemeal but exceedingly forceful way, depending largely on the potency of the European interests present in a particular region. Sir John Seeley, the founding father of British imperial history, echoed Palmerston when he claimed that 'the British Empire was acquired in a fit of absence of mind'. The point that he was making was that there had been no central blueprint for empire, no 'Plan of Global Dominance' approved by a British Cabinet—just incessant, ad hoc growth on the peripheries. In contrast, Harry Flashman, the gutless and philandering soldier-hero of George MacDonald Fraser's novels, had quite a different perspective on British imperial expansion, expressed in typically coarse fashion. 'Absence of mind, my arse', he declared. 'We *always* knew what we were doing; we just didn't always know how it would pan out.' His was the view from the colonial coalface, the view of the empire-builder not the armchair historian or the Whitehall-bound official. Fraser's point is that it was *'presence* of mind' on the part of Britons overseas that led to imperial expansion, even if they could not foresee where their actions would lead. Presence of mind, he said, but also 'countless other things, such as greed and Christianity, decency and villainy, policy and lunacy, deep design and blind chance, pride and trade, blunder and curiosity, passion, ignorance, chivalry and expediency, honest pursuit of right, and determination to keep the bloody Frogs out'. As a summary of the motive forces of British imperial expansion, MacDonald's list is hard to better. Philippa Levine criticizes the overplayed assertion that the British built an enormous overseas empire by accident, or only did so reluctantly. Absent minded, perhaps, but inexorable and frenetic too: even at its most 'absent minded' the British Empire, like Topsy, 'just growed', and the extent of its overseas conquests and the diversity of the situations in which it fetched up as the ruling power was quite breathtaking.

The law of unintended consequences meant that missionaries who arrived in some distant land to convert people often achieved hardly any conversions at all, but an awful lot else. Their work might transform political dynamics and undermine the authority of indigenous rulers; it might transfer new agricultural and medical ideas and skills, develop literacy and education and, by dint of this, nationalism, as many later nationalists learned to read and write and argue using Western texts and concepts whilst being educated by missionaries. Missionaries stimulated the rise of African churches in opposition to their European progenitors. They provoked cultural resistance that could feed political nationalism, empire's nemesis, such as when they sought to interfere with Kikuyu circumcision practices, to the chagrin of the colonial administration. Missionary teachings caused Hong Xiuquan, leader of the Taiping Rebellion that killed about twenty million people, to believe that he was the younger brother of Jesus Christ and to found the Heavenly Kingdom in south China. None of these things were intended by the mutton-chop whiskered missionaries and their loyal catechists, but they all resulted from their efforts to convert people to Christianity.

Examples of the law of unintended consequences abound. Captain Cook's reports of large whale populations off Antarctica caused British whalers to hunt them, decimating their population. The spread of firearms traded by concessions-seekers or businessmen weaponized internal disputes in newly fatal ways that destabilized regions and caused imperial interventions. British interventions in India, relating to caste and customs such as suttee (the self-immolation of widows) made Hindu caste structures more salient, not less. The development of communications infrastructure such as railways, ports, and shipping lines enabled people to complete the hajj and forged new networks of trade in a world that was becoming more interconnected, also allowing opponents of empire to become more vocal and more effectively mobilized. Like a bullet ricocheting off multiple surfaces, it was difficult to predict how Europe's initial contact with diverse regions and peoples would play out, though it was safe to assume that nine times out of ten it would lead to further colonial encroachment.

The actions of individuals, organizations, and governments

Whilst imperialism is a process, the British Empire was created by sentient human beings acting upon the world around them—Europeans, but also the indigenous people who treated with them, resisted them, traded with them, and allied with them. There were numerous impulses causing individuals, organizations, and governments to 'do things' overseas. The desire for resources and money-making opportunities was paramount in the initial phases. There was then the drive to leave the British Isles and start life anew elsewhere, through compulsion or choice. Monarchs and governments perceived the need to compete with

10. Forts and factories on the coast, early roots of empire in India. Plan of the Citadel of Calcutta and Fort William, the East India Company's Fortified Warehouse, *c.* 1750 (pen & ink & watercolour on paper), English School (18th century)

rival states through territorial acquisition. The impulse to proselytize and to civilize heathens and to improve or restore their cultures was potent, and the quest for knowledge of the world and all its wonders became an obsession. All of these motives found ready numbers of Britons desperate enough, rich enough, inspired enough, or intrepid enough to act upon them.

In most parts of the world that became red on the map, European agents—botanists, consuls, traders, military officers, missionaries, explorers, settlers, even artists—had been operating for significant periods of time *before* formal rule was declared. Thus East India Company men and their proxies were operating in India, largely on sufferance, generations before the company (and by extension, Britain), controlled anything beyond tiny coastal enclaves. Similarly, Europeans were active in the African hinterland decades before there were any formal British colonies or protectorates there; David Livingstone, for instance, visited Lake Ngami forty years before the declaration of the protectorate of Bechuanaland that it became a part of. Likewise, Thomas Baines was painting baobabs and scenes of the Zambezi three decades before the foundation of Rhodesia, and prospecting for gold in Mashonaland two decades before Cecil Rhodes' 'pioneer column' came and raised the flag. The activities of these individuals have been interpreted as 'hollowing out' places for later colonial rule, drawing attention to exploitable resources in a particular area, publicizing problems that might strike a chord with missionaries or humanitarians, or contributing to instability that eventually called forth metropolitan attempts to sort out the mess—pedalling whiskey and guns, perhaps, or creating communities of Christians that threatened chiefly authority and that were in turn connected to powerful lobbies back in Britain that might, for the sake of 'saving' a region from Arab slavers or some other dastardly threat, implore the government to act. In a range of ways these activities forged the interface between Britain/Europe and other regions and cultures. It was individuals, often backed by institutions and companies, who were to the fore in this penetration; the likes of Richard Burton, Robert Clive, James Cook, George

Goldie, George Grey, David Livingstone, Frederick Lugard, William Mackinnon, Alfred Milner, Stamford Raffles, Cecil Rhodes, Edward Gibbon Wakefield, and Arthur Wellesley were formidable empire-making machines, schwerpunkts of colonialism that proved to be quite irresistible. Behind them stood geographical and learned societies, large companies and institutions such as museums and botanical gardens, military force, powerful backers in Whitehall and the City, flourishing missionary societies, chambers of commerce and industrialists, an interested and occasionally proactive public, and sometimes the British government itself. Their endeavours begot further endeavours: explorers explored, then broadcast to the world what they had found and the opportunities it offered; missionaries did the same, messengers of grace just as they were harbingers of imperial rule. They offered the prospect of desirable places to live and to take, desirable resources to harvest, reports of new pastures crying out for good works or packed with potential customers requiring, if only they knew it, shirts from Lancashire, teacups from Stoke-on-Trent, and the Word of the Lord.

The formal declaration of a new colony, therefore, was usually a post-facto action after agents on the ground had effectively 'softened up' an area and made it, in the memorable words of the renowned imperial historians Ronald Robinson and Jack Gallagher, a fruit 'ripe for the plucking'. What they meant by this was that the declaration of formal colonies often came at the *end* of a lengthy process of interaction between indigenous societies and colonial elements that had usually been to the detriment of the former and the benefit of the latter. Colonial rule, on this reading, was often at least partially caused by the need to halt and discipline uncontrolled elements of Europe's invasion that had contributed to or caused instability and disruption.

Settler states soon developed minds of their own (as did the viceroy of India) and this often led them to undertake ventures such as appropriating land or declaring war on neighbouring states of which Whitehall and Westminster disapproved, though rarely to the point of bothering to do anything to reverse them. This was especially the case in the days when even basic communication between here and 'over there' took weeks or months rather than minutes, and when there was in practice little that London could do if a rash viceroy invaded Tibet or colonists in Australia mistreated the native population. Frequently, the 'man on the spot', or the settlers on the spot, called the tune, not the pipe-masters in distant London. So, too, did private companies such as the East India Company and the British South Africa Company. Missionary societies could also have a surprisingly powerful say in whether or not a Pacific island or an inland region of Africa became British, especially once they had mobilized their vocal lobbyists back at home.

What of the role of the British government then? It was government that shaped the environment in which imperial factors could operate, and it was only the government that could 'officially' create colonies even if it was the forces of private enterprise that provided the energy on the ground. Even if it sometimes despaired of them, the government usually underwrote private imperial advances, often presented with a fait accompli or a situation that might go embarrassingly wrong unless a colony was declared. The British state played a crucial role in affording protection to settlers, facilitating the operations of chartered companies or colonization societies, whilst the emerging global economy enabled new settler societies to become solvent. Government ministers were often helpless bystanders as agents overseas—larger-than-life figures such as Bartle Frere, George Curzon, or Cecil Rhodes—kept adding new bits to the Empire. In the literature, such proconsuls and adventurers are referred to as the 'man on the spot', their empire-building activities, and those of settler communities, termed 'sub-imperialism'.

But in significant cases, imperial expansion came at the direct behest of the British monarch or, following the monarchy's eclipse by parliament, the British government. *Government-led* empire-building, when it occurred, was driven by geopolitical factors and the desire for wealth, and was particularly prevalent in the seventeenth and eighteenth centuries and again from the 1880s as the government sought to shore up the untidy expansion of the previous half-century. It needed to better its rivals, to consolidate its overseas position, to secure crumbling frontiers, to build strategic bases, and to heed the cries of merchants concerned that Britain would be cut off from potential riches if rivals were allowed to monopolize a particular region. The dictates of strategy, particularly related to the defence of sea routes and of India, and pre-emption of rivals or reaction to their colonial gambits, were an important impulse, adding territories such as the Cape, Cyprus, Egypt, Gibraltar, Griqualand West, Jamaica, Malta, Mauritius, the Seychelles, the Swahili coast, and Zanzibar to the Empire. British governments also perceived a need to formally extend their sovereignty over British settlements, unless they come to consider themselves beyond the law or became magnets for opponents of the British state.

In cases of state-led expansion, a significant impulse was the desire to compete with other monarchs, states, and churches, or troublesome locals such as the Boers in South Africa. There were a number of reasons for this, including prestige, the quest for strategic advantage, religious pride, dynastic advancement, and the accumulation of wealth. It did so as Britain competed with European rivals—particularly Holland, France, Russia, and Spain—power struggles that involved trade wars across the oceans of the world and the acquisition of enemies' colonies because of their economic or strategic value. International competition swelled imperial bounds in places such as the Caribbean, Central Asia, and during the partitions of Africa and the Pacific, and government sanctioned forward moves in order to pre-empt those of rivals, 'pegging out claims for the future', as the sometime Prime Minster Lord Rosebery termed it.

Situations in which there was an element of *conjunction* between the interests of the British government and private forces 'on the ground' were those that were most likely to lead to the declaration of a colony or protectorate. Thus the government might sponsor geographical expeditions up the Niger or applaud British South Africa Company or London Missionary Society activities in Central Africa because they helped forestall the expansion of rivals. The government might commission privateers ('pirates') to shoot up Spanish trade in the West Indies, or use East India Company forces to fight the French.

Maritime requirement, war, and strategy

Britain's imperial presence in a region often began for reasons of maritime requirement, with no thought to the hinterland expansion that, nevertheless, tended to follow in its wake. When they first landed, the British were usually gazing out to sea, not looking greedily inland, and the fact that coastal enclaves developed into large colonies should not obscure the reason why they were obtained in the first place. British holdings in West and South Africa, for example, began on the coast for reasons of resource exportation (slaves) and maritime strategy (Cape Town's position on the sea route east). In neither case was there any ambition to carve out inland colonies. The British clung on to the coast like limpets for the first century and a half of their time in India. Likewise, the British arrived in Ceylon because Trincomalee provided an excellent harbor for naval operations, which had to be both utilized and denied to the enemy. It was only later that the British began to expand inland, to a large extent sucked inwards by the kingdom of Kandy's habit of raiding Britain's coastal settlements. Likewise, British rule settled upon islands such as Mauritius and the Seychelles for no other reason than the need to secure ports and anchorages for the use of the Royal Navy rather than the naval forces of Britain's enemies.

The Empire also expanded through incessant frontier warfare. Settler communities always rubbed uncomfortably against their borders and were prone to violent and acquisitive expansion as soon as their strength allowed. It was a story repeated the world over, as bridgeheads expanded, settlers pushed the frontiers, colonial governments sought buffer zones in order to insulate colonies from threats that lay beyond, and indigenous polities sought to involve Europeans in their own internal disputes or contested their presence, usually leading to war and inland expansion. These activities established turbulent frontiers in regions previously unconnected to Europe, and created multiple interfaces between Britons and overseas societies that often developed into imperial relationships.

War and strategy were central to the growth of the British Empire. It was built and secured through wars fought against European rivals and local states—usually involving significant indigenously recruited manpower. The British state's effectiveness in war was crucial to its imperial expansion, and between 1790 and 1830 Britain engaged in an extensive period of warfare and empire-building which transformed its position as an imperial state, established its reputation as a global military power, and secured its naval pre-eminence. Strategic rivalry, sometimes pursued through offering loans or railway technology to semi-dependent rulers, was a constant source of imperial expansion and competition. Wars against great power rivals, as has been seen, added vast tracts of territory to the British Empire—including the Middle Eastern territories gained from the Ottoman Empire during the First World War, and scattered German colonies in Africa and the Pacific. The number of wars fought against indigenous polities, from small-scale 'punitive raids' and frontier 'skirmishes' to campaigns involving scores of thousands of troops and camp followers, was astonishing. Colonial warfare became commonplace, part of the background noise of an expanding empire; violence, repression, sometimes even atrocity were integral to imperial expansion.

Trade and commerce

The desire for resources was both the chicken and the egg of British imperial expansion. Settlements that became colonies were often founded because of the desire to access raw materials—foodstuffs (fish, molasses, sugar, tea, coffee), drugs (opium, tobacco), fuels and minerals (diamonds, gold, oil), fabrics (fur, cotton, jute, silk), metals (tin, copper), natural products (ivory, ostrich feathers, palm oil, rubber, sandalwood, teak), and much more, including strategic naval supplies such as flax which allowed Britain to be self-sufficient in times of war. In decreeing that goods sailing between British and colonial ports could only be carried in British vessels, the government ensured that it had a plentiful supply of seasoned seamen and a merchant marine from which it could requisition ships in times of war (enshrined in the Navigation Acts, intended to protect British markets from ruinous Dutch and Spanish competition). The trading needs of the East India Company led it to establish settlements in places such as Aden, Penang, Singapore, and Surat, either because of their value as trade entrepôts or as strategic bases from which to protect shipping against pirates. The profusion of trading companies at this time offers a clue to the early origins of Britain's overseas empire. There was the Royal African Company, set up in 1660, which had a monopoly on slaving and was led by Charles II's brother. The Levant Company was formed in 1581 to supervise British trade with the Ottoman Empire and the Levantine outlets of the overland route to Asia. Alum, spices, and wine were imported from the Mediterranean, English cloth sent thither. The Muscovy Company was founded in 1555, the Virginia Company in 1606 to found settlements in the Americas, chartered by James I. The South Sea Company (1711) was created to conduct trade with Spanish America. The British Empire was a network of resources and markets connected to Britain and defended through the occupation of strategically placed islands, peninsulas, and coastal regions. With the coming of industrialization, Britain was able to achieve something unique – to create a coherent global economic system that could integrate even the most distant regions.

Religion

The British Empire also grew through Protestantism. Anti-Catholicism spurred British empire-building and Protestantism shaped the British Atlantic world from the Reformation to the American Revolution. It united the Atlantic world whilst simultaneously sowing religious diversity and fragmentation. The Reformation involved a clash of peoples and beliefs in England, Scotland, Ireland, parts of North and South America, the Caribbean, and Africa, and fuelled colonial expansion as bitter rivalries prompted fierce competition for souls. Despite officially promoting religious homogeneity, the English found it impossible to prevent the conflicts in their homeland from infecting their new colonies. In the eighteenth and nineteenth centuries, a major theme relating to empire, in terms of migration, expansion, and cultural relations, was the growth of powerful missionary societies and humanitarian activism. Most famously this was associated with the abolition of slavery, an endeavour that continued late into the nineteenth century as the desire to defeat, for example, the Arab slave trade, provided a new rallying call for missionary activity and colonial expansion to underwrite it.

Settlement and migration

According to some scholars, 'settlerism' was a more important process in the 'Anglobalization' of the world than imperialism per se. The 'cloning' of British society, to use James Belich's term, was the most significant process in modern history. The peopling of Australasia, North America, and South Africa with Britons and other Europeans was part of a global movement, one characterized by 'mutual exploitation' between the metropole and the nascent overseas societies, and the forging of voluntary ties. Emigration, supported by the state (and then the settler states), went from being perceived as a disastrous choice to being viewed as a desirable one. Outward migration from the British Isles, and the consequent creation of vigorous new settler societies that expanded the boundaries of the Europeanized world, was one of the defining features of the British Empire. The settler colonies were unique to the British Empire in terms of their size, and a central aspect of its capacity to construct global ties of ethnic and economic complementarity and add a thick Anglicized layer to the character of entire geographic regions.

Settlers were possibly the most effective and, from the point of view of indigenous society, pernicious engine of imperial expansion: not without reason was the term 'white plague' adopted. As Magee and Thompson remind us, 'Territorial expansion was as much demographic as it was bureaucratic, religious, or military', with over fifty million people leaving Europe between 1850 and 1914. Emigration underpinned new divisions of labour in the international economy and triggered an exodus of people from Asia to work in British colonies around the world. Settlers were like clockwork mice; wherever they were set down, they moved off across the land, veering erratically to the left or right but rarely ceasing to move. They conquered America and Canada from east coast to west, moved inland from their settlements on the Australian coast to take over the continent, and trekked inland from the Cape towards the Orange River.

There were many motives: Britain was widely perceived to be overpopulated, so settlement received powerful intellectual and official support though there was, especially in the eighteenth century, opposition from politicians and landowners. The enclosure acts had forced many people off the land and into the expanding industrial cities, and poverty and the prospect of gaining status through landownership persuaded many to move abroad. Others were fleeing from persecution, or were forcibly moved, as convicts transported to New South Wales or Irish rebels dumped in North America. There was then the official transplantation of settlers in order to claim territory for Britain and protect nascent colonial states, occurring in places such as Ireland, Jamaica, and South Africa. Some migrants yearned for adventure or to convert 'heathens', others were attracted by advertisements from fledgling settler states attempting to populate the vast 'empty' spaces of Canada, increase the British stock in Southern Rhodesia, and lure people to New Zealand, 'the Britain of the South'. There were then the schemes of colonization theorists such as Edward Gibbon Wakefield and their societies such as the Canterbury Association, seeking to create 'model' colonies overseas, whilst gold rushes in Australia, Canada, and South Africa offered the prospect of getting rich quick.

Empire oversaw other significant migrations too. The Atlantic slave trade transported twelve million people from Africa to the Americas and the West Indies. Between 1707 and 1807, Britain shipped about 30,000 of these slaves per annum, a gargantuan exercise in social engineering. There were countless smaller migrations too, such as the Indians sent to Uganda to build the railway or the steady trickle of Sikhs who accompanied the British around the world as policemen. There was also a great deal of internal migration as, for example, hundreds of thousands of Africans from all over Southern-Central Africa were involved in the labour migration cycle that manned the gold mines of the Rand. Often, the communities affected were missing up to 50 per cent of their adult males, as they were part lured and part forced to enter the cash economy by the twin demands of consumerism and the need to pay taxes. Afrikaners trekked inland to form states in the Orange Free State and the Transvaal in an attempt to escape British rule.

The abolition of slavery caused the growth of another system of exploitative labour known as 'indentured labour'. Drawing mainly on India and China, it led to the growth of new communities in distant places such as Fiji (where Asian and Chinese immigrants came to outnumber the indigenous population), as well as Malaysia, Mauritius, South Africa, and Trinidad. As the British Empire disintegrated after the Second World War, employment shortages in Britain led to mass migration from South Asia, sub-Saharan Africa, and the West Indies to the 'mother country' itself, as did specific events such as Idi Amin's ejection of Asians from Uganda and the countdown to the handover of Hong Kong to China in 1997.

Having considered the most salient drivers of British empire-building, the following chapter charts the story of the Empire's global expansion and its demise in the twentieth-century.

Chapter 4
Rise and fall

The British Empire grew in stages over the course of many centuries: from 'internal colonization' within the British Isles in the Middle Ages to seventeenth-century growth in North America and the West Indies, through phases of expansion in South Asia and Australasia in the eighteenth-century, and in Africa, the Pacific, and South-East Asia in the nineteenth-century. A final flourish of empire-building occurred in the Middle East in the early twentieth century. The Empire's character shifted over time, from an original emphasis on settler communities and a mercantile economic system to a multi-ethnic, global conglomeration powered by an industrial economy.

Notwithstanding its island status, Britain was always connected to wider worlds: to Ireland and continental Europe, and across the waters of the Atlantic to Africa, the Americas, and beyond. Britain itself had been colonized by invaders, most completely by the Romans and the Normans. Just as Britain's history cannot be understood without reference to these overseas connections, the history of the British Empire cannot be understood without reference to the wider international setting. The British Empire was an integral feature of the wave of European expansion that transformed the world, and was always an empire among empires. The tides of global history governed its fortunes, and whilst British governments might have been able to influence them,

71

never, even at the height of Britain's power, were they able to control them. Tellingly, when other European empires began to crumble, the writing was on the wall for Britain's sprawling imperial edifice too; the European empires rose and fell together.

Historians have written of a 'first' British Empire all the way to a 'fourth' in seeking to describe the changing nature of imperial power and the shifting geography of the imperial estate. The first British Empire was largely destroyed by the loss of the American colonies, followed by a 'swing to the east' and the foundation of a second British Empire based on commercial and territorial expansion in South Asia. The third British Empire was the construction of a 'white' dominion power bloc in the international system based on Britain's relations with its settler offshoots Australia, Canada, New Zealand, and South Africa – the original Commonwealth club. The fourth British Empire, meanwhile, is used to denote Britain's rejuvenated imperial focus on Africa and South-East Asia following the Second World War and the independence in 1947–8 of Britain's South Asian dependencies, when the Empire became a vital crutch in Britain's economic recovery.

The British Empire grew from salients established by soldiers, sailors, traders, and adventurers, and in the interstices of empires in decline (such as the Chinese, Moghul, Ottoman, and Spanish). It grew through successful competition with rival empires, some of them, such as the Burmese, relatively small, localized, and weak, others, such as the French, global and capable of challenging Britain economically, politically, ideologically, and militarily. Even at its zenith, the British Empire was constantly buffeted by the claims of rival empires or would-be imperial states, as well as the centrifugal forces generated by independent-minded settlers, nascent nationalists, and traditional leaders unwilling to accept the manifestations of colonialism and determined to reject the baleful effects on their power and their culture that often trailed in the wake of the arrival of the first white men (or red men, as they were described in some parts of the world, more accurately reflecting their skin colour under the tropical sun).

Origins of empire to the seventeenth century

Internal colonization forged the British nation as the English subdued and partially fused with the Irish, the Scots, and the Welsh. Involving subjugation but also elite collaboration and cultural assimilation on all sides, the birth of Britain created a potent colonizing force. From as early as the reign of Henry I, son of William the Conqueror, scholars have identified the conceptualization of a British Empire, the formation of a British state and identity synonymous with the emergence of an imperial ideology. Anglo-Norman attempts to conquer Ireland began in the twelfth century, though it was not until the sixteenth century that English authority was made good beyond its original Dublin bridgehead, sometimes known as The Pale. English conquest of neighbouring realms involved deeply unsavoury elements of colonization such as land alienation, ethnic persecution, and cultural chauvinism, features which were to become depressingly familiar in the Empire's subsequent extension overseas.

It could take decades, even centuries, before a coastal enclave became a stimulant of hinterland expansion and eventual dominance. The extension of English rule across the whole of Ireland took centuries to be made good (though it was never free from internal insurrection) and involved nothing less than a war on Irish culture and the Catholic religion, and the granting of huge tracts of Irish land to 'loyal' Irishmen and veterans of Oliver Cromwell's parliamentary army. Ireland had the double misfortune of being, after the Protestant Reformation, both the seat of a despised religion and strategically located; enemies often put troops ashore to ally with the Irish and threaten England from close in, and as late as the Second World War the fear remained of the enemy appearing at the gate. The kingdoms of England and

Scotland warred sporadically until the eighteenth century, though the 1707 act of union saw the two countries merge to form Great Britain, joined by Ireland in 1800.

Beyond the British Isles, the seeds of empire were planted in the Mediterranean as Britain engaged in imperial and religious conflicts and sought to develop trade and trade routes, the security of which involved periodic expeditions against the 'Barbary pirates' of North Africa. In the late fifteenth century temporary settlements and trading posts began to form on the other side of the Atlantic. John Cabot, a Genoese acting on behalf of Henry VII, reached a 'newe founde land' (Newfoundland) and from this point on Englishmen attempted to exploit its resources. Formal claim to the territory was lodged by Sir Humphrey Gilbert in 1583 in order to support fishing and hunting activities, but the French also established bases there. A year later, Queen Elizabeth I granted Sir Walter Raleigh a charter to establish a settlement in what became Virginia, motivated by the desire for New World wealth and ports from which to attack the Spanish, leading to an abortive attempt to settle on Roanoke Island. With spices such as cloves becoming fashionable at the Elizabethan court, expeditions were sent even further afield, around the Cape and across the Indian Ocean in an attempt to challenge the Portuguese monopoly and get a share of the lucrative trade developing in the East.

Raleigh, eventually executed for treason, was typical of the freebooters who built the Empire. Gilbert's half-brother, he twice set sail in search of the fabled 'El Dorado' or 'City of Gold' in South America, and committed acts of piracy against the Spanish. Early voyages to the New World marked British participation in European exploration—the attempt to discover a 'north-west passage' to Asia—as well as the search for plentiful stocks of fish and fur. Though often enjoying royal patronage, early attempts at exploration, settlement, and trade were down to the private citizens of places such as Bristol, Exeter, London, and Plymouth. Royal patronage was particularly important in this early and definitive phase of imperial expansion as English society was transplanted across the Atlantic. This is reflected in the range of places named for monarchs (Virginia, Maryland, Williamsburg, Jamestown, Georgia, Charleston, Carolina). Monarchs were keenly interested in progress and anything that would further the ambitions of the state, sponsoring initiatives such as the Royal Observatory (1675) and navigational research as they encouraged advances in science, technology, and discovery. They were also prepared to grant trading monopolies to private companies and gift vast tracts of other people's land to relatives and favourites. British activity in the New World was also driven by fear of Catholic nations and the desire to prevent them from using its resources to defeat the Protestant kingdoms. No fewer than six major wars were fought with European rivals between 1689 and 1815. The Protestant Reformation unleashed forces that augmented existing imperial initiatives and created new ones, including the perceived need to secure the state against hostile Catholic powers, and the desire of individuals to proselytize and convert non-Europeans.

As well as beaver pelts, cod, maritime exploration, and fear and loathing of Catholics, the developing Atlantic empire was based upon slaves and consumer crops. It rested on the development of a triangular trade which saw slaves transported from West Africa via the 'middle passage' to the plantations of America and the West Indies. The proceeds from the sale of the slaves were used to buy slave-produced cash crops (cotton, sugar, tobacco, rum), which were then loaded into the slave ships and sent to Britain for sale, or for re-export to other European markets. These imports shaped the tastes of a new consumer society, and re-exports increased foreign earnings. From the 1750s until the 1820s, sugar was Britain's biggest import. The third side of the triangle was formed by manufactured goods (guns, beads, cloth) travelling from Britain to West Africa, where they were used to purchase slaves. This was the definitive feature of the first British Empire. By the end of the eighteenth century North America and the West

Indies took 57 per cent of British exports and accounted for 32 per cent of British imports.

The first major essays in extra-European colonization and settlement took place in the Americas and West Indies (named so

LONDON'S VIRGINIA.

11. Plantation owners take their ease while slaves toil in the tobacco field; English woodcut, c. 1700, used as a tobacco package label

because Columbus thought he had sighted Asia). In 1607 the first successful settlement on mainland America was established at Jamestown, which was saved from extinction by the development of tobacco as a cash crop and the hospitality of the local people. Plymouth was founded in 1620 by the puritan 'Pilgrim Fathers' and Maryland was settled by Catholics in 1634. By 1640, 20,000 people had emigrated to New England. New Netherlands was taken from the Dutch in 1664, its capital New Amsterdam renamed New York. This gave Britain a vital strategic foothold, central to other mainland colonies and well placed to vie with France for dominance of the vast region that would one day become Canada. In 1681 Charles II granted William Penn an enormous tract of land in settlement of a debt owed to his father, thus founding the state of Pennsylvania. Towns such as Dover and Portsmouth grew as centres of the lumber trade supplying the navy with masts and staves for the West Indies. The Hudson's Bay Company was chartered in 1670 to compete with the French and make money from the fur trade, and until the coming of formal British colonial rule and the creation of Canada it acted as a de facto government, at one time the largest landowner in the world. By the end of the seventeenth century, around 400,000 people had left Britain for the Americas and the West Indies. Wherever settlements grew, engagement with the indigenous population developed, vacillating between uneasy coexistence and outright hostility.

Whilst Wellington might have thought he had the scum of the earth in his army during the Peninsular War, a fair proportion of them had already found their way to the islands of the Caribbean and the American seaboard. Slaves and silver were the big attractions in the Caribbean; John Hawkins from Plymouth attempted to break into the Africa-Caribbean slave trade in 1562, and Sir Francis Drake's raid on a Spanish silver train from Panama in 1573 made his name. Settlements in the Caribbean (Guiana, Grenada, and St Lucia) failed in the first decade of the seventeenth century, but succeeded in Bermuda, settled by the

Virginia Company in 1609 and not taken over formally as an official British colony until a hundred years later. St Kitts, Barbados, and Nevis were settled in the 1620s. Jamaica was taken from the Spanish in 1655 as part of Cromwell's Western Design aimed at securing bases in the West Indies to interdict Spanish treasure and challenge Catholicism in the New World. The Bahamas were settled in 1648 by the Puritans who went on to establish New Providence, and in 1667 Cromwell granted the East India Company a charter to establish a fort on St Helena, a way-station in the South Atlantic. In 1622 the company helped the Persian shah attack the Portuguese fort-cum-factory at Hormuz, yielding Britain a toehold in the Gulf as the shah rewarded their alliance with a factory at Bandar Abbas.

In West Africa, Britain possessed coastal forts employed in the operation of the slave trade. James Island on the River Gambia was used by the Royal Adventurers in Africa Company from the start of the seventeenth century as a base for the ivory, gold, and slave trades. Further demonstrating the multifarious roots of the British Empire, the seventeenth century also brought imperial accretions through dynastic intermarriage. Bombay and Tangier were gifted to the English crown as part of Princess Catharine of Portugal's dowry upon her marriage to Charles II in 1661, to be developed as naval stations and centres of commerce. The Glorious Revolution that brought William of Orange to the throne in 1688 de-escalated growing competition between Britain and Holland, and brought about the demarcation of agreed 'spheres of influence', Britain gaining primacy in India, the Dutch in the East Indies. As the more vigorous power, however, there was little that could be done to prevent individual British actors from muscling in on the Dutch trade, irrespective of the agreement in place between the governments. A similar situation was later to pertain in South America, where British actors' paid scant regard to Spain's supposed monopoly of the region's trade. This was business, and it was cut-throat. Transoceanic trade, the search for resources, and the need to compete with rival states drove imperial expansion. It was a world increasingly shaped and connected by the activities of Europe's seaborne imperial powers Britain, France, Holland, Portugal, and Spain.

Planting the seeds of what would grow into significant British activity in another part of the world, in 1600 the East India Company was founded, its royal charter granting it a monopoly of all trade east of the Cape of Good Hope. It was an unashamed attempt to make money for individuals and for the state from the lucrative trade in eastern commodities such as spices and textiles, fuelling Britain's competition with the Dutch, the then dominant power in the region, as well as the Portuguese. It was the classic imperial story of economic and strategic fusion. Illustrating the role of unintended consequences in the history of the Empire, the company was formed with the intent of trading with the famous spice islands—the 'East Indies'—though ended up becoming the dominant presence on the subcontinent which lay to the north.

The eighteenth century

Holland and France, as well as Britain, were emerging on the global stage to challenge the position of Portugal and Spain, Europe's pioneer imperialists in the Americas, Africa, Arabia, India, South-East Asia, and the East Indies. Developments in maritime and weapons technology enabled small units to travel across large distances and take on indigenous peoples. Wars in the seventeenth and eighteenth centuries amongst these rivals saw Britain establish a dominant presence in the Caribbean and the Americas and also in Asia where, trading to places such as Surat, it sought to displace its rivals and cash in on valuable trade routes. Britain's economy, benefiting from the industrial revolution, became the strongest in the world, and upon this bedrock the British Empire developed as a system of global economic production and exchange, its vitality and security augmented by the growing pre-eminence of the British navy and the development of powerful settler communities which gave the British Empire an in-built complementarity between the 'mother country' and its overseas offspring.

The eighteenth century witnessed the continued growth of British colonies in America. Georgia, named after the king, was established in 1732. The last of the thirteen colonies, it was developed as an experimental agrarian society. Rivalry with France dominated proceedings in North America during the eighteenth century, the two empires facing each across ever narrowing frontiers, as trade and emigration brought more of the continent under European sway. At this time French enterprises, centred on Montreal and Quebec, were larger than those of the Hudson's Bay Company.

Whilst often focused on European dynastic disputes, the wars of this period usually had naked ambition for trade and territory at their core. They were global conflicts, in which if (for example) Britain was fighting Spain, it was just as likely to attempt to sack Manila or interdict enemy shipping in the Caribbean as it was to take action on Spanish soil itself, or if fighting France, to play out the contest in the Ohio valley. During these conflicts, the ever-pragmatic British government would frequently sanction the activities of pirates and privateers as long as they were directed against the ships and possessions of Britain's enemies, and often had occasion to make use of individuals such as the pirate Henry (later Sir Henry) Morgan as governors and proconsuls.

As a result of the War of the Spanish Succession (1710–14) Britain gained Acadia, the French part of Newfoundland, the Spanish half of St Kitts, as well as Gibraltar and Minorca. One of the main causes of the Seven Years' War (1756–63) was colonial and trade rivalry between Britain and its enemies France and Spain, as well as tensions within the Holy Roman Empire, giving its military and naval campaigns twin European and extra-European dimensions.

Through victory Britain reaped new colonies in the Caribbean and evicted the French from North America, bringing French Canadian provinces within the Empire's bounds. It also gained Florida from Spain, advanced its position in Bengal, and degraded the French position in India to such an extent that British dominance of the subcontinent could follow unhindered by the interference of external rivals operating alongside internal proxies. British strategy in such wars involved blockading enemy states and interdicting their trade, taking advantage of British seapower to shunt troops around the world to attack enemy colonies and keep open the trade routes linking overseas centres to home. The eighteenth century witnessed a significant change in the Empire's composition. It had been, other than the African slaves that it contained and indigenous populations, predominantly conceived as an empire of white settlement, and that largely Anglo-Saxon. With the acquisition of French Canada, the Empire inherited its first set of disgruntled non-British whites, and with the rash of conquests in India, it obtained an enormous non-European population too, prompting people in Britain to debate the nature of this phenomenon.

Whilst war led to a constant expansion of British territory overseas through asset-stripping rival empires, *internal* factors simultaneously 'made good' sweeping territorial claims elsewhere. Wherever there were settlers, they ceaselessly pushed forward the frontiers of the Empire. In North America they drove westward towards the Pacific coast, whilst in India, the power of the East India Company grew as the Mughal Empire declined and the company sought security and revenue through expansion. It became enmeshed in local political dynamics and disputes that led inexorably to its transformation from a trading company into an aggressive colonizing force.

The East India Company operated from main trading settlements in Bombay, Calcutta, and Madras, shipping goods from Asia worth up to one million pounds a year. In Bengal the company traded under the aegis of a local dynasty which it came increasingly to control; the Madras presidency, where Britain had purchased land for forts and factories in the 1630s, expanded; and Bombay came into conflict with the powerful Maratha states surrounding it. Thus the East India Company became entwined in Indian politics, and attempted to exploit its position to further its own ends and hamper those of the rival French company. It gave military aid to friendly states in return for trade concessions. In the process states in the Carnatic and elsewhere became British puppets. In Bengal, the British battled with the nawabs, themselves weakened by the extent of British penetration. In 1756 the nawab (governor) of Bengal, Siraj-ad-Daula, wrested control of Calcutta from the British, leading to the famous 'black hole' incident. The nawab's success was short-lived, and he was driven out the following year by Colonel Robert Clive at the Battle of Plassey, a victory won through conspiracy between the British and members of the nawab's court and Indian bankers. This conflict was the culmination of the company's forceful attempts to gain trade concessions. Succeeding nawabs were removed when they failed to meet East India Company demands and it became much more like a British colony. This was symbolized when the nawab granted the company *diwani*, the right to raise revenue and administer finances, in 1765.

The mid-eighteenth century was definitive. Before, Britain had confined its imperial endeavours to the Atlantic world, only venturing overseas to lodge factories on the flanks of indigenous empires and kingdoms. Now, it ventured beyond the Atlantic world bringing settlement and rule. The 'military-fiscal' state took a grip on India. The events of the 1750s and 1760s heralded the establishment of the 'Bengal bridgehead' from which further expansion would follow—even though further expansion was expressly forbidden by London. Britain's representatives on the ground, such as Robert Clive, Warren Hastings, and Arthur Wellesley, were prepared to take the offensive on flimsy pretexts and with scant regard for doubts emanating from distant London, claiming the need to do so for defensive reasons. The company was seeking to establish its own paramountcy and defeat potential rivals. Thus it warred against Mysore until it was broken, and the kingdom of Awadh was turned into a client state in order to safeguard Bengal. The process provoked other Indian powers, such as the Marathas, and this led to further war and conquest, the prospect of security and more tax revenue propelling governors-general forward, illustrating the power of the man on the spot to make empire, even in defiance of the metropole. In 1803 Wellesley (the future Duke of Wellington) defeated the Marathas at Assaye, the East India Company dominating the military labour market and starving the enemy of troops. A pattern of border wars aimed at securing the company's growing estate took shape as the company became locked into a cycle of conquest followed by financial crisis resulting in further conquest as revenue was ruthlessly run to ground. In the 1770s and 1780s it needed financial help from the government, which in return imposed stricter controls upon it, beginning the company's transition from a private business into a branch of the imperial estate.

Despite Britain's growing international power and its success in the inherently imperial warfare of the period, it did not have things all its own way. In 1776 the American colonies declared independence after defeating the British on land, whilst at sea the intervention of the French navy, deployed by a rival desperate to see Britain undone wherever possible, proved decisive. Sea routes and the capacity to employ sea power, in defence of trade and in order to project power on land, was vital to the British Empire and its system of imperial defence. On this rare occasion Britain lost that control of the sea on which it depended in a vital region at a vital time, and thus America was lost; without French naval intervention, General Washington would have been unable to trap Lord Cornwallis at Yorktown, the decisive battle of the American War of Independence.

But just as the British were being ejected from America, they were establishing a new colony of settlement in Australia and opening up new vistas onto the Pacific world. It had long been thought that a large fertile continent existed around the South Pole, and there was still no resolution as to whether or not there was a north-west passage connecting the Atlantic and the Pacific. Captain James Cook went to find out, and to observe the transit of Venus across the sun. In 1770 he discovered (for the British; its inhabitants already knew about it) and charted the east coast of Australia, claimed it for Britain, and named it New South Wales. He also claimed the north and south islands of New Zealand, and was killed on Hawaii Island in 1779. Reports from Cook's scientific and exploratory voyages, including the drawings of the botanist Joseph Banks, advertised the range of opportunities offered in Australia and the Pacific. It was not long before they were acted upon, and in 1788 the 'first fleet' of eleven British ships arrived at Botany Bay, bearing 1,000 free people and convicts, with the express purpose of colonizing this part of Australia. 'What Frobisher, Raleigh, Delaware, and Gates did for America', said Governor Arthur

12. **Illustration from *The Voyages of Captain Cook* (watercolour on paper), by Isaac Robert Cruikshank (1789–1856)**

Phillip to the assembled colonists after they had landed, 'we are this day met to do for Australia'.

The nineteenth century

The sub-imperial activities of the East India Company transformed the surrounding region as India became an imperial power in its own right, emitting expansionist waves as far east as China and as far west as East Africa. British interests in South-East Asia, the Persian Gulf, the Red Sea, Arabian peninsula, and East Africa were driven from India. The subcontinent stood at the centre of an emergent system of global trade, investment, migration, and security. It was India, the twin pillar of the Empire, which allowed Britain to dominate the entire Indian Ocean region. As the nineteenth century opened, tea was the company's most valuable export, traded from Canton and paid for by the sale of Indian goods to China (as was silk). Cotton from Bombay had been to the fore, but soon opium shipped from Calcutta began to take over. It was an illegal trade, but the fact was that although China accepted some woollen and cotton goods in exchange, it did not want much that the British had to offer, and they were reluctant to pay in bullion. So, opium it was. The East India Company pioneered Britain's early links with South-East Asia, seeking a trading entrepôt that would allow it to operate and compete effectively with European rivals. This led initially to the establishment of a British settlement on Penang Island in 1786. But George Town, named in honour of the king by its founder, East India Company man Francis Lightfoot, was soon eclipsed when the strategically placed island of Singapore was taken in 1819 by another East India Company man, Stamford Raffles.

The loss of America coincided with significant growth in British territory and influence in Asia and the Pacific, and Britain's long-standing rivalry with France came to a head in the Revolutionary and Napoleonic Wars. As with the previous conflicts, this prolonged period of warfare (1792–1815) witnessed a classic blend of European causes and actions—at one time Napoleon had an invasion force ready to cross the English Channel—and global confrontations. French and British land forces and their proxies engaged in set-piece battles in India as well as the Netherlands, Portugal, and Spain; British troops invaded Ceylon, Java, Mauritius, Rodrigues, and the Cape in order to oust their enemies or prevent Dutch territories falling to them. French and British commanders vied for Malta (taken by the British as a naval redoubt in 1814) and fought in Egypt, and commerce raiding and the defence of convoys became the keys to war at sea, in the Atlantic, the Indian Ocean, and the Mediterranean. In all of this fighting, proxy forces drawn from the colonial world and huge amounts of indigenous labour were crucial to military operations. The British Empire grew once again on the spoils of war, most of its colonial gains formalized at the subsequent peace treaties. A new era of autocratic, military government—colonial despotism—opened as an 'authoritarian conservative nationalism' took hold, along with a new vision of empire which equated it with moral improvement and a 'providential expansion of civilization'.

The defeat of Napoleon set the stage for an unprecedented period of peace—the so-called 'pax Britannica'—and British pre-eminence. Of course, it was not real peace; an extraordinary range of colonial conflicts formed a backdrop to the helter-skelter expansion of the British Empire. But it was a period of peace in the sense that from 1815 until 1914 the British only fought one great power—Russia in the Crimean War, a conflict with distinct imperial dimensions, British participation prompted by fear that Russia was encroaching on the weakening Ottoman Empire and might soon gain access to the Mediterranean.

The colonization of Australia continued apace. Over 160,000 convicts reached New South Wales before transportation ceased in the 1840s, and the numbers of free settlers increased year on year, the more fortunate of whom received grants of free land and convict labour to work it. Gold strikes enticed people to the diggings, causing the rapid growth of the colony of Victoria. New colonies were founded in Australia as British interests and claims spread out from the original New South Wales settlement. Tasmania was declared a separate colony in 1825, Western Australia was claimed by Britain three years later, and new colonies were created in South Australia (1836), Victoria (1851), and Queensland (1859). Men such as Edward Gibbon Wakefield and John Godley propagated new communities in both Australia and New Zealand. They were part of an influential movement to form 'model' societies, God-fearing and structured according to social hierarchy ranging from squires to labourers, away from the increasingly urban and industrialized British homeland. Private enterprise and the church drove settlement in New Zealand, and the influential New Zealand Company received the backing of the British government, which annexed the country to mitigate lawlessness and head off a possible French claim. These vigorous new settlements, which soon developed the capacity to outmatch and subdue the indigenous peoples, became jumping off points for people exploring the wider Pacific world in search of produce, or labourers, or fresh fields for missionary and humanitarian endeavour.

Britain's presence in India continued to grow too, Sind conquered in the 1840s, the decade in which the Sikh wars made the Punjab British. Awadh was annexed in 1856. A war was fought in Afghanistan (1839–42) as Britain tried to shore up India's northern border and anticipate Russian expansion from Central Asia, the Gurkha War (1814–16) was fought to protect the border, and Britain was also active in Iran. From India the 'empire of the Raj' expanded, resources from the subcontinent furthering Britain's presence in the Gulf, annexing Aden in 1839 as a strategic base, intervening in Egypt in 1801, mounting an expedition to release British consuls in Abyssinia in 1867, and developing the Uganda Railway as East Africa was 'opened up'. On India's eastern borders, three phases of warfare (1820s, 1850s, and

1880s) brought British rule to the entire kingdom of Burma. In 1841 James Brooke became the rajah of Sarawak on the island of Borneo, and nearby Labuan was taken in 1846 as a base for anti-piracy operations in the South China Sea and a link on the sea route east.

Britain's and Europe's engagement with China also developed in this period, an immensely important aspect of nineteenth-century global history. Uninterested in Britain's industrial wares and dismissing the need to engage with this 'barbarian' power, Chinese officials had spurned British advances. But in the Opium Wars (1839–42 and 1856–60) Britain led the charge to 'open up' this insular kingdom, as it sought—through violence, if necessary—to access the products that it wanted and to ensure the 'free trade' importation of those it had to sell, such as opium. It was a measure of the West's technological superiority over a declining empire, of British naval supremacy and overbearing commercial vigour, and of Britain's leadership of a process of imperial penetration that was very much a Western (as opposed to solely British) phenomenon. From these engagements emerged the treaty port system, which allowed Europeans privileged access to numerous Chinese ports and cemented the 'impaired sovereignty' that the Chinese state endured until the Second World War. Britain gained Hong Kong in 1841 and Kowloon, opposite Hong Kong Island on the Chinese mainland, in 1860 (its extension north of Boundary Road, the New Territories, leased in 1898). Britain became the dominant power in Shanghai, and the Hong Kong and Shanghai Bank (1864) and the Royal Navy's China Squadron, which included gunboat flotillas policing China's inland waterways, became instruments of British power and influence in the region. Further indicating Britain's influence in China, British personnel ran the Imperial Maritime Customs Service, the Chinese state's main revenue-gathering structure.

The Empire expanded relentlessly throughout the nineteenth century. The Royal Navy garrisoned Ascension Island in the Atlantic from 1815, and nearby Tristan da Cunha was annexed the following year in order to deny its use to enemies in times of war, one of many examples of negative annexation. Britain's roots in Africa long pre-dated its formal colonial presence though extensive inland penetration of the 'dark continent' had been discouraged by physical barriers and disease. An early British foray into sub-Saharan Africa was the foundation of a settlement for freed slaves—Freetown—in what became the colony of Sierra Leone. The first freed slaves landed in 1787 and African American ex-slaves began to arrive in the following decade. Freetown was annexed as a crown colony in 1808, and became a base for naval operations against the slave trade after its abolition. Bathurst in Gambia was established in 1816 as a trading post and base for anti-slavery operations. A colony from 1821, it was also used for the wax and hide trades. The British had some trading forts in the Gold Coast, and the development of the palm oil trade led to increasing interest in the region of the Niger, Lagos being taken in 1861. Thus British commercial and other activity was widespread in West Africa throughout the early nineteenth century, with numerous coastal colonies declared and upriver explorations and trading missions, though it was not until later in the nineteenth century that the inland contours of colonies such as the Gold Coast and Nigeria took shape.

In Southern Africa, Britain took the Cape from the Dutch in 1806, to the chagrin of the Dutch settler population, established there since the 1650s. In 1788 the African Association was founded and became a focal point for exploration of the Niger and the source of the Nile. Other agencies, such as the Royal Geographical Society, missionary societies such as the London Missionary Society and the Universities' Mission to Central Africa, and chartered companies, also became important sponsors of European penetration of Africa. Some expeditions were government backed and geographical enquiry merged with evangelism in the form of explorers such as David Livingstone. Expansion in South Africa was a drawn-out process in which disputes over land, labour, and cattle led to many wars between African polities and settlers sometimes backed by British troops. Colonial authorities were unable to control local conflicts or establish firm frontiers. Even here there was concern over French expansion which, along with the latest effort to close off Boer expansion, led to the annexation of Natal (1842).

It took over a hundred years before what became the Union of South Africa was fully demarcated, after prolonged struggles with indigenous African peoples (such as the the Khoi Khoi, the Pedi, the Xhosa, and the Zulus) and conflicts with the Boer republics which did not want to become part of Britain's expanding imperial realm and against whom they fought wars in the 1850s, 1880s, and 1890s (the most significant of which, the Anglo-Boer War of 1899–1902, witnessed the deployment of nearly half a million imperial servicemen). Most of Britain's large African empire was acquired in the late nineteenth century during an extraordinary period often referred to as the 'Scramble for Africa'. British expansion in this period occurred in Central Africa, East Africa, and West Africa, including holdings in the Horn of Africa with the establishment of British Somaliland and the conquest of the Sudan in 1898 as Britain sought to secure its position in Egypt and dominate the headwaters of the Nile. British imperialism in this region was driven forward by state-sponsored exploration, clashes with the French, and the new geopolitical significance of the region since the opening of the Suez Canal, considered a key strategic thoroughfare by the British government.

Africa was not the only region 'scrambled' for by European colonial powers in the late nineteenth century. Though, like Africa, the roots of Britain's presence were considerably older, in both South-East Asia and the Pacific the late nineteenth century witnessed a frenetic scramble brought on by European competition. British possessions in Malaya grew exponentially, as did its stock of Pacific islands. Since early exploration, Europeans had had a devastating effect upon the Pacific. Missionaries often provided succour to societies dented by the activities of traders, whalers, deserters, escaped convicts, labour hunters, and the like, though sometimes were themselves part of the 'fatal impact' interface between previously isolated peoples and the chaotic modern world. Lawlessness—European lawlessness—prevailed; disease was widespread; labour trafficking became a major problem. The coming of more formal colonial rule was in part a reaction to this growing chaos, as well as the British government's response to the forward moves of other imperial powers in the region. The new High Commission of the Western Pacific (1874) was designed to control the activities of British subjects (though in practice it lacked the resources to do so effectively). Towards the end of the nineteenth century, America, Germany, and Japan joined Britain and France in claiming islands in this ocean. Britain's share included the Solomon Islands, the Gilbert and Ellice Islands, Tonga and numerous others, the high commission being based in Fiji.

New colonies and protectorates were acquired all over the world. The Central American territory of British Honduras was created in 1862; Cyprus was taken from the moribund Ottoman Empire in 1878 as the British government watched Russia's penetration towards the Mediterranean with anxiety. North Borneo became a British territory under a trading company in 1882, and Brunei a protectorate in 1888; and in 1881–2, Britain began a takeover in Egypt that heralded a 'temporary occupation' that lasted until the 1950s, motivated by the drive to secure, for British shipping, trade, and strategic interests, the newly cut Suez Canal. In the latter half of the 1880s, charters were granted to the Royal Niger Company, the British South Africa Company, and the Imperial British East Africa Company, as private individuals and their businesses sought to develop economic resources in the African hinterland, and to develop shipping lines connecting

Britain with the main imperial regions, such as the Peninsular and Oriental Steam Navigation Company and the British-India Steam Navigation Company with its extensive operations in the Gulf and the Indian Ocean.

The middle years of the nineteenth century were the pinnacle of Britain's global power. It was confident in its ability to shape the world in its own image and in the desirability and righteousness of doing so; it was prosperous and in the vanguard of a developing global economy; and its growing Empire was complimented by 'informal' relations with certain regions of the world where it did not feel the need for conquest and direct rule because it could achieve its ends without them, by dint of its power and its ability to coerce and cajole. But the aberration that was Britain's unrivalled global position in the mid-nineteenth century was being eroded all the time. Imperceptibly at first, the tectonic plates of global power were shifting. Having seen off its main imperial rivals (France, Holland, and Spain), it was now challenged by new ones. America grew rapidly as an economic power, as did Germany, newly united in the 1870s and hungry for an empire of its own. Other powers unified, industrialized, and began to look beyond their own borders, for resources, for territory, and for prestige. Even weak powers, such as newly united Italy and newly created Belgium, wanted to get in on the imperial act. Russia, like France, continued to challenge Britain's position, and from the late nineteenth century Japan sought to develop its power in the international system. All of this meant a more crowded imperial field and increased the chances of clashes between rival countries and their traders and military personnel. This climate encouraged speculative and pre-emptive land grabs in order to deny potentially valuable regions to rival powers. It made the British government declare formal colonies in regions such as East Africa where, hitherto, informal means had been sufficient to safeguard Britain's interests. It also led to international (i.e. Western) conferences aimed at diffusing tension and marking out spheres of influence around the table in

European chancelleries—which had the spin-off effect of stimulating the activities of concession hunters and other nationally badged actors, whose claims or activities were often used as 'proof' of a British, say, or a German claim to a particular patch of real estate in far-off Africa or the Pacific. The most famous of these meetings was the Berlin Congo Conference of 1885, though there were numerous bilateral agreements in this period, such as the 1890 Zanzibar-Heligoland Treaty in which Germany agreed to respect Britain's 'sphere of influence' in Zanzibar and the portion of the Swahili coast that its Sultan claimed to rule, in return for the British territory of Heligoland, an archipelago in the North Sea that Britain had taken from the Danes in 1807 as a base for operations against Napoleon.

Britain reacted to the rise of new imperial powers by pegging out its own claims more firmly in regions that Britain had come to regard as its own 'spheres of influence', contributing to the pace of colonization towards the end of the nineteenth century. The 'new imperialism', a term coined to capture the heightened sense of conscious concern about Britain's imperial position leading to jingoism and forward moves to beat off challengers, saw the British become more imperially minded than ever before, and to identify the country's own 'greatness', security, and prosperity with its vast imperial holdings overseas. It was based further on concerns about the economy (the 'great depression' lasted from the 1870s until the 1890s) and Britain's global competitiveness, the search for new markets blending with the 'el dorado' appeal of new continents being opened up. Not only was Britain's economic lead being cut as other nations industrialized and developed as military, trading, and financial powers, but the burdens of defending the Empire eroded its position further. It begged the question: did empire make Britain stronger or weaker?

The twentieth century

In the twentieth century Britain made significant territorial claims in the Antarctic and acquired a sizeable new empire in the Middle East on the back of the defeat and disintegration of the German and Ottoman empires as a result of the First World War. Britain gained Iraq, Palestine, and Trans-Jordan as League of Nations mandates as well as numerous former German possessions in Africa and the Pacific, some of them administered by Australia, New Zealand, and South Africa, eliciting the remark that now 'even the colonies had colonies'. Once again, 'European' wars turned out to be intensely imperial and, once again, the Empire grew as a result of British victory, pyrrhic though in many ways it was. Britain's exploration in the Antarctic during the first decades of the century was a symptom of growing imperial rivalry in the region and a mark of Britain's intent to make good its claims there. Though there were to be some minor tweaks to the imperial estate after this and temporary jurisdiction over other countries' colonies as a result of the Second World War, this latter phase of expansion represented the high water mark of the British Empire.

The world wars of the twentieth century, whilst born of European causes, were, like their eighteenth- and nineteenth-century predecessors, inherently imperial. Indeed, in addition to their European causes, in both cases they were also partly caused by the desire of 'have not' powers such as Germany, Italy, and Japan to catch up with their neighbours and develop resource-rich empires of their own. Though ending on the winning side in both struggles, they sapped Britain's economic power and encouraged new forces that themselves were solvents of European imperialism. The First World War entrenched the 'moral disarmament' of empire. European triumphalism and confidence in its superiority had been shaken to the foundations by the epic proportions of the slaughter. Both world wars also involved millions of colonial people as male and female service personnel, merchant navy sailors, and civilian labourers. For the British

Empire, the Second World War was a catastrophe. A victor power in 1945, Britain was nevertheless enervated by the political and economic costs of six years of conflict which had witnessed vast swathes of its empire conquered by the Japanese, and the surrender of British economic independence to America.

British decolonization took off in 1947–8 with the independence of its South Asia colonies (Burma, Ceylon, India, and Pakistan). Palestine was returned to the United Nations in 1948, though Britain's departure from this corner of empire illustrates the fact that there was no decolonization 'domino effect'; the situation leading to Palestine's relinquishment differed entirely from that pertaining in India, and was unique. There were then no further decolonizations until the mid-1950s. The significance of the Suez Crisis in 1956 was that it was a punitive expedition in fine old colonial style that failed. The episode painfully demonstrated the new global reality in which America called the shots, and showed that high-handed imperial actions were no longer suitable to the Cold War situation. By all means, undermine or replace recalcitrant 'developing world' leaders (the Americans and British had engineered Mossadegh's removal in Iran a few years before), but do it more discreetly. Having been ejected from Egypt, the Sudan was logically given independence in the same year. Ghana, the former Gold Coast, was the first 'black' African country to become independent, in the same year (1957) as Malaysia had its 'merdeka' moment (initially including Singapore). The next major decolonization period was the early to mid-1960s, when most of Britain's African territories gained their independence. It was a decade characterized by Lancaster House constitutional conferences and flag-lowering ceremonies as a procession of new states took their bow on the international stage: Aden, Barbados, Botswana, Cameroon, Cyprus, Gambia, Ghana, Guyana, Jamaica, Kenya, Lesotho, Malawi, the Maldives, Malta, Mauritius, Nauru, Nigeria, Samoa, Sierra Leone, Somalia, Swaziland, Tanzania, Trinidad and Tobago, Uganda, Zambia, and Zanzibar.

But decolonization did not end there, and dozens more colonies, mainly small islands in the Caribbean and Pacific previously considered too small to become viable nation-states, became independent in the 1970s, even into the 1980s. The old white states of Africa, where the settlers had become the rebels, took longer to decolonize than the rest of Africa: Rhodesia did not finally give way to Zimbabwe until 1980 and South Africa, which had left the Commonwealth in 1961 as a protest against Britain's anti-apartheid stance, did not shed white minority rule until 1994. Hong Kong, the last 'big' colony, was handed over to China (rather than becoming independent) in 1997.

Though decolonization is most strongly associated with the post-war period, particularly from 1945 until the mid-1960s, decolonization was not a new phenomenon. On the one hand, the British Empire had endured a significant bout of decolonization (as had the Portuguese and Spanish empires) in the eighteenth century with the loss of the American colonies. Furthermore, Britain had been *demitting* or *devolving* measures of power to its white settler colonies since the mid-nineteenth century and, from the First World War, to India too, particularly through the 1917 Montagu–Chelmsford reforms and the 1935 Government of India Act (reforms intended in the best British tradition of 'reform in order to preserve' to prolong Britain's rule in India, not hasten its demise). Interestingly, because of the lengthy process by which the 'white' dominions became independent, they never had the flag independence moment that non-white colonies enjoyed. The point is that, even when there *was* 'flag independence'—India and Pakistan's moment in 1947, for example, or Basutoland's transformation into Lesotho in 1966—the processes that had gone into making those moments had roots in the past.

Just as the *arrival* of British rule on a certain date of formal acquisition does not tell the story of the years, sometimes decades, of invasive colonial activity in that territory beforehand, so it is with the coming of independence. Thus the ways 'out' of empire were nearly as varied as the ways 'in' had been, though there were certain broad background factors common to most individual incidents of decolonization. These occurred at the level of the international system (Britain's declining power vis-à-vis other countries; the decolonization of other empires; the rise of powerful anti-colonial bodies and ideas; and the principle of the right to self-determination). They occurred at the level of the British state (economically bankrupt; declining as a trading nation; struggling to meet the military and other costs of maintaining empire whilst developing a welfare state at home). And they occurred at the level of the colonies themselves (where nationalism fomented more rigorous resistance to alien rule, through sophisticated political movements or armed struggle).

The Empire went into decline as the environment ceased to be permissive. This occurred once people in Britain began to question the morality or practicality of empire and its associated costs in blood and treasure; once the international climate of opinion became anti-imperial and pro-nationalist; once the political, ideological, and physical means of resisting empire became more widely available; once maintaining empire became politically, economically, militarily, and morally expensive; and once supranational bodies such as the United Nations, along with 'anti-imperial' superpowers, rose to prominence and the media became more intrusive. When these forces came to a head in the 1940s and 1950s, empire became unviable. The cost of having and holding a large territorial empire became too great to bear. Ergo, it had to go.

Competition and interaction among empires remained an important factor governing the British Empire's fate; whilst the actions of weak empires, such as the Portuguese, impacted upon Britain's decolonization strategy (there was a reluctance in Whitehall to be left in the last ditch with the Portuguese, widely perceived to be particularly backward colonialists), so too did the rise of two new super-empires, America and the Soviet Union. These two powers were reordering the imperial contours of the world, marking out a new landscape of satellites and proxies, one in which old-style European colonial rule was not welcome. On some readings, the decolonization of the European empires was little more than a footnote to the emerging Cold War with its deadly game of nuclear call-my-bluff. Old-style colonial rule was increasingly 'out'; but this did not for a moment mean that countries such as Britain were abandoning their ambitions to influence and steer weaker polities, and there was a strong hope that a British-led Commonwealth would emerge, not quite the old Empire, but nevertheless a British-directed bloc, distinct from the American or Russian blocs and a real presence on the world stage. Old habits die hard, and in the 1950s Britain did not want to give up its world role or its position, say, in the Middle East, despite the increasingly tenuous and threatened nature of that presence. The game was to try and manage Britain's declining power, harbour resources, and turn rule into influence. Independence settlements might not have been ideal, but then, it was not an ideal world, and options were usually limited. Leaving Malaysia and Singapore as viable pro-Western, anti-communist, nations that were 'open for business', for instance, was considered something of an achievement.

The need to divest oneself of colonies because of their unpopularity with increasingly vocal nationalists and the sentiments of previously voiceless non-Europeans, and because of their unpopularity with Washington, Moscow, and the United Nations, was a crucial backdrop to decolonization. Old colonialism was no good for fighting communism, an urgent imperative of Britain's senior ally across the Atlantic, but one felt in Whitehall too, where the Foreign Office (for example) often cursed the Colonial Office's 'parochialism' and resistance to the rules of the new game that made maintaining a colonial empire small beer in comparison to preventing the spread of communism and fending off a nuclear Armageddon. As the Colonial Office

strove to resist the UN and its anti-colonial machinations
and failed to see the need to work with the Americans, the Foreign
Office ploughed a different furrow, indicating how easy it was for
institutions on 'the same side', such as partner ministries of state,
to envision the 'national interest' in markedly different ways.

After the Second World War the overriding focus of successive
British governments was the attempt to recover Britain's economic
independence, destroyed by the costs of war, and to defeat the
global menace posed by communist Russia whilst cementing its
strategic alliance with America. Holding on to colonies was
relatively unimportant given these dominant themes, especially
when set against the backdrop of the nuclear arms race and the
threat of annihilation. Winning the ideological struggle was vital,
and if this meant giving independence to new nations and hoping
that they remained within the Commonwealth club and the
Western orbit, then so be it. The Commonwealth, traditionally the
preserve of the 'white' dominions, became a useful tool for
attempting to shepherd emerging non-white nation-states into a
post-imperial but still British-led club, given its emphasis on
progress towards self-government. It provided the British with
something to hold up to the international community—look at us,
we are developing colonies to nationhood!—a cunning piece of
opportunism as the British claimed that they had always meant it
to be this way, as if, indeed, the whole imperial enterprise had had
eventual self-government and independence as its aim following a
necessary period of tutelage.

The British were impressively sanguine about their ability to pull
off the conversion of Empire into a British-led Commonwealth of
Nations, evincing blithe confidence when looking to the future.
It was hoped that the Commonwealth would not only be a
good answer to charges of 'colonialism', but also a useful,
British-directed instrument of Western influence in the fight
against communism—in fact, the British Empire updated for the
mid-twentieth century—and therefore a plausible alternative to

the growing narrative of British decline. The British believed that they could manage and channel nationalism, and that even when they departed and a new national flag was hoisted, they would continue to be able to nudge and influence a country. It was even hoped that independent India would remain part of the club, which did not transpire as India chose to make its own way in the world and became a pioneer of the 'non-aligned' movement. Though not without its successes, Britain's desire for a shadow empire of economic and political influence to replace the formal one foundered on the rocks of economic decline, closer integration with Europe, and the unwillingness of newly-independent nations to do Britain's bidding. That said, through political, economic, intelligence, and defence links, many former colonies retained a significant attachment to Britain.

Ironically, whilst being one of the main solvents of the British Empire because of its professed anti-colonialism and its commercial penetration of previously protected British spheres, America actually became a buttress of Britain's imperial position. In the 1950s and 1960s it saw Britain as an important ally, and the Empire as a valuable bloc of 'allied' states that might otherwise become communist. In the late 1960s, as Britain announced its withdrawal from 'east of Suez', America beseeched Britain not to disengage from the last region where the British held sway.

Chapter 5
Writing the Empire story

Empire has been a powerful theme in British and postcolonial literature, and was once a central feature of the British national story taught to schoolchildren and consequently embedded in the national conscience. Imperial and wider world themes were encountered in a vast array of adult and children's literature, from *Our Empire Story Told to Boys and Girls* (1908) to the pages of public school-inspired comics such as *Chums*, the news coverage of the British press, and the novels, poems, and short stories of Kipling, Rider Haggard, G. A. Henty, Conrad, and Somerset Maugham. Imperial themes and ideas appeared in a host of literature that purportedly had nothing to do with the British Empire or an imperial world view, including such favourites as *Cider with Rosie, Swallows and Amazons, The Secret Garden, Vanity Fair*, Flora Thompson's *Lark Rise to Candleford*, A. E. Housman's *A Shropshire Lad*, and the novels of Evelyn Waugh.

As for historians, scholars working on geology and sanitation, prostitution and disease, human rights, and the history of beer and railways have all contributed to knowledge about the British Empire. In fact there are few areas of historical enquiry that the study of the British Empire can be left *out* of: whether studying the history of one of the many countries that were part of the Empire (including Britain itself) or the history of a particular geographical region, it is impossible not to encounter the British

Empire. The same is true of topics such as the global economy, the history of industry and technology, race relations, and the evolution of the nation-state and global communications. The history of tea, chocolate, and narcotics are entwined with the history of the British Empire, as is the history of Christianity and sport. Important new fields have been brought into contact with 'mainstream' imperial history, such as gender, environmental studies, and the cultural dimensions of empire, and the recovery of indigenous accomplishments has been a major preoccupation since the end of colonial rule. An important thread in the composition of imperial history has been woven by the memoirs and diaries of former district officers and others 'who were there' which have appeared in abundance in recent decades. These complement and contrast with the works of people displaced by empire or who fought against it or came to deplore its contradictions, a heterogeneous field including people such as Franz Fanon, Mohandas Gandhi, J. A. Hobson, V. I. Lenin, Linton Kwesi Johnson, V. S. Naipaul, George Orwell, Bob Marley, George Padmore, Edward Said, Leonard Wolfe, Mary Kingsley, and Kwame Nkrumah.

During the days of empire, economists from Adam Smith onwards debated the virtues or otherwise of empire as thinking on mercantilism and free trade developed in the late eighteenth and early nineteenth centuries. Charles Dilke in *Greater Britain* (1868) argued that the settler communities of British stock and Britain itself formed a vital economic and political bloc, an Anglo-Saxon world. James Froude claimed that English society was unique in spreading national values and beliefs through empire. Imperial history as a distinct discipline emerged in the late nineteenth century, marked by the publication of texts such as John Seeley's *Expansion of England* (1883) and the establishment of a professorial chair at Oxford in 1905. The story of Britain's rise as a global power became a standard part of school history texts and national self-image. The focus of early works on the Empire was on Britain's imperial achievement, the flavour distinctly Whiggish, taking for granted Britain's position as a force for good in the world. British imperial power was seen as the culmination of Anglo-Saxon superiority, and history was about how Britons won the world and made it a better place. The 'great men' of empire were lionized. In 1908 J. W. Willis, Education Chairman of Worcester County Council, wrote that the school curriculum should:

> bring before the children the lives and work of English people who served God in Church and State, to show that they did this by courage, endurance, and self-sacrifice, that as a result, the British Empire was founded and extended and that it behoved every child to emulate them.

As the discipline of imperial history developed it concentrated on elites, the story of white achievement, and colonial administrators

13. British Royal Marines landing in Sierra Leone, 2000. Despite successive waves of defence cuts since the 1950s, the British military retains a 'global reach' and global outlook, as well as overseas bases in places such as Cyprus, the Gulf, British Indian Ocean Territory, Singapore, the Falklands, Northern Ireland, and Brunei

and explorers. Empire-builders were rarely anything other than heroic, intrepid, patriotic, noble, and admirable role-models. What most interested Europeans was themselves; a history of trade and diplomacy, invasion and conquest, heavily infused with assumptions about racial superiority. For the period following conquest, colonial writing focused on the progress of administrative structures, transport networks, and business enterprises. Missionaries and explorers published accounts of their travels that were widely disseminated, as were accounts of overseas endeavours in the popular press.

Apart from the story-telling of popular culture, as a field of academic research imperial history became wrapped up in constitutionalism and the achievements of the Empire's 'great men': until the 1960s it had very little to do with indigenous people, except when they resisted British rule or allegedly benefited from it. The Empire's subject peoples were largely passive; the imperial story was 'our' story, not theirs. Hugh Trevor-Roper famously decreed that Africa had no history prior to the arrival of Europeans; it was nothing more, he wrote, than the 'unedifying gyrations of barbarous tribes in picturesque but irrelevant corners of the globe'. African history now, of course, is a vigorous discipline in its own right, epitomizing the rise of 'area studies' (interdisciplinary studies focusing on particular geographical regions) which fractured the former 'certainties' and elegant contours of a version of world history dominated by empire.

In the 1950s and 1960s economic historians questioned the causes of British expansion, some finding them in the investment of capital overseas that then drew on government protection in the form of colonial rule, whilst others developed theories about expansion being driven by strategic needs. Jack Gallagher and Ronald Robinson introduced the concept of the 'non-European foundations' of empire. This supplanted earlier approaches by arguing that imperialism was as much a function of its victims' collaboration and non-collaboration—of their indigenous politics, their willingness to cooperate with colonial impositions or fight against them—as it was of European expansion. This was part of a revolution in the writing of imperial history that coincided with the collapse of the European empires and the urgent need for new histories—especially for newly independent nations as they sought to imagine their own futures through the study of the past, and to come to terms with the colonial interlude in their societies' history. It also witnessed the rise of the idea that colonial rule had 'underdeveloped' vast stretches of an emerging 'third world', and been the source of pernicious 'cultural imperialism'.

From being overwhelmingly metropolitan in focus, prone to an Olympian 'top down' approach and preoccupied with political, economic, and strategic questions, history 'from below' became increasingly common, a new generation emphasizing 'subaltern' studies—the attempt to recover the 'voice' and 'agency' of indigenous subjects. Answering the question 'what is imperial history now?', Linda Colley argued that imperial history demands a wide scope, both geographically and chronologically, and attention to the connections created by empire on a global scale. It is 'impossible to consider a single empire, such as the British, outside the universe of other empires with which it competed, collided, and collaborated. Nor is it possible any longer to tell the history of empire as if from the centre, with the synoptic eye of a metropolitan administrator.'

A better marriage between 'British history' and 'British imperial history' has been affected in recent years, including a proper understanding of the Empire's impacts upon Britain, its economy, society, and culture. 'Imperial' themes, such as the history of America and Ireland, of slavery, migration, and the domestic impact of empire now pervade metropolitan (British) scholarship. This reflects inevitable progress in the accumulation of knowledge and the fact that views on empire—and instances of empire—have changed markedly. So too have the questions that successive generations have sought to ask the past. These trends have added immeasurably to our understanding of what the British Empire was and what it meant to the hundreds of millions of people who lived within its bounds. Developments in the study of the British Empire represent a natural evolution, as scholars in one generation stand on the shoulders of their predecessors, critiquing and augmenting their work with promising perspectives from other branches of history and other disciplines.

The debate about what the British Empire meant for its subjects is intense and emotive. For some authors, the Empire's historical headline is its role in making the modern world. Though it had its attendant evils, they would contend, it was on the whole a progressive force in human affairs. Those who adopt this position are often keen for the British to 'stop apologizing' for their Empire, even to celebrate its achievements. Niall Ferguson recently argued that the Empire had made the modern world and left a host of beneficial legacies, and that America needed to become more consciously imperialistic in order to preserve the international order. Empire created an international system of free trade facilitating exponential growth in the world economy. It promoted free movement of capital and labour and bequeathed useful legal and administrative principles beneficial for growth, providing order and protecting property in an impartial manner.

Opponents of this view see it as problematic, ethically suspect, and wallowing in the nostalgia of an illusory past 'greatness' and skewed Western notions of 'progress' and the beneficence of contact with the Western-developed global economy. They would counter that 'development', where it occurred, was always conducted with the intention of lining pockets and developing Britain, or was conducted in a piecemeal and limited way at the margins of affordability as colonial governments worked within a system constrained by 'balanced budget' parsimony. B. R. Tomlinson suggests that the Empire did not leave a substantial legacy of health, wealth, or happiness. Some scholars hold that the empire was responsible for keeping the world's have-nots in a state of deprivation and sullying their identities. Those favouring this approach argue that the Empire was a phase in a continuing story of Western capitalist domination, manifest today in a 'liberal imperial' project that pursues the same old goals. Academic histories of the British Empire walk the tightrope between these two extremes.

In the second decade of the 21st century, the writing of British imperial history is characterized by vigorous debate, a constant stream of fascinating new case studies, and interpretations of the imperial past in the light of current world events. Grand narrative histories of the Empire remain in vogue, sometimes accompanied by television series. Favourable interpretations of the Empire and its legacies vie with those documenting its pernicious effects. The British Empire is increasingly 'de-centred' and examined in the light of transnational and global histories. And a 'new imperial history', influenced by post-colonialism and post-modernism, has both challenged and argmented more orthodox accounts of the kaleidoscopic phenomenon that masquerades behind the phrase 'the British Empire'.

Chapter 6
Legacies

This chapter examines some of the legacies of the British Empire, including the debate about whether it was a 'good' or a 'bad' thing, which itself is one of its salient remnants. Observing Aden's independence ceremony in 1967, the British High Commissioner Sir Richard Turnbull told the Defence Secretary Denis Healey that the Empire would only be remembered for 'Association Football and the term "fuck off"'. Whilst football and colourful expletives were definite bequests of British imperialism, there are other, more substantial legacies too, many of which continue to have relevance in a world shaped by the 300-year phenomenon of Western global dominance. Whatever one's view on the merits of studying the history of the British Empire, or opinions about whether it was a good or bad thing, the point is that it so profoundly shaped the world that knowledge of its impact is important if we want to understand why things are the way they are in the world we live in today.

International legacies

The impact of the British Empire (and European imperialism more generally) was even more profound than the visible legacies of empire etched into the international system alone would suggest. Legacies of the British Empire are woven into the fabric of the modern world, in phenomena such as the state system, the international maritime order, international law, and the mental attitude of many people towards, say, Africa or abstract notions such as 'development'. The British Empire influenced so many aspects of the world that it is surprising we do not hear more about its legacies. For a start, it created new countries, most with national boundaries that are peculiar because of the unusual geographical extent of the land they envelop and because of the ethnic and cultural heterogeneity of that which they contain. In Africa, ruler-straight boundaries running for hundreds of miles mark out enormous countries, their unity, such as it is, stemming from colonial divisions worked out in the chancelleries of Europe and therefore completely alien (it is estimated that nearly 200 'tribal' territories are divided by international borders, which nevertheless have proven to be surprisingly durable). Canada is an over-sized country born of settler expansion, colonial struggles between Britain and France, and the British Empire's internal processes of amalgamation. So too is Australia, a single country covering an entire continent by virtue of the federation of a number of disparate settler colonies formed at different times and for different reasons. The United Arab Emirates is a conglomeration of the seven emirates formerly known as the Trucial States. Malaysia is a single country spread across the Malay peninsula and, 500 miles away, the island of Borneo, where over 60 per cent of its land mass lies. South Africa meanwhile is a union of four former British and Afrikaner colonies that might just as easily have developed as a number of separate white-dominated states. Nigeria is a loose envelope thrown around a mass of diverse ethnic, linguistic, and religious groups. India owes its unity to the processes of imperial expansion and imperial rule—in other circumstances, the subcontinent might well have been a conglomeration of separate states based on the powerful kingdoms that emerged during the decline of the Mughal Empire. Hong Kong and Singapore are quintessential creations of British imperialism, and in the Arctic, the Antarctic Treaty System is a simmering legacy of the colonial order.

The international system, therefore, remains heavily marked by the hand of British imperialism, and the borders, nations, and federations it created. Within these borders, many of the problems that continue to capture headlines were generated, exacerbated, or left unresolved by British rule. Whilst the period of British rule was not *solely* responsible for their problems, many former British colonies were endowed upon independence with regional, ethnic, and political challenges that inform them still. We might consider the travails of Iraq, or the Quebec issue in Canada. The Kashmir dispute is another obvious example, as too are the divisions between north and south in countries such as Nigeria, or the fractured status of Somalia, not helped by its division amongst no fewer than five colonial powers. Colonial boundaries such as the 1,600-mile-long Durand Line separating Afghanistan and Pakistan, or that dividing Sudan and the newly created state of South Sudan (2011), remain live political issues exercising the minds of politicians, strategists, UN Secretary-Generals' special representatives, and aid workers. So too do differences between 'host' ethnic communities and those 'imported' under colonial rule, such as Tamils in Sri Lanka, Indians in East Africa, and the Rohingya in Burma. The 'garrison state' in Pakistan continues to inform its post-independence history, and Egypt has had to deal with the legacy of the 'military extractive' state created to help Britain use it as a base from which to fight its wars and secure its regional interests.

The British Empire, and more specifically the government at its apex, never 'controlled' all of the processes over which it presided or with which its pre-eminence was coterminous, any more than today's powerful nations or supranational bodies initiate, direct, or control global movements in spheres such as climate change, disease, economics, migration, or technology. Rather, they are buffeted by them. Recessions, epidemics, famines, and violence have always been phenomena that individual governments, no matter how powerful, are at the mercy of and react to. This is the case even if their policies have sometimes (and usually unwittingly) helped cause them or exacerbated their effects, and even though they are rightly looked to for amelioration and even solutions.

The nation-state is one of the main legacies of European imperialism, particularly visible in the modern world in cases of state 'failure' or 'collapse'. The nation-state is not, of course, bad per se, despite Basil Davidson's memorable label 'the black man's burden'. Some former colonies have become successful states. But the state apparatus was often erected in colonies that were simply not ready for it following hasty decolonization (it worked well in rare cases, such as India, where indigenization of the upper echelons of the bureaucracy and officer corps had been steadily taking place for decades before independence). Democratic institutions and practices were installed haphazardly and rapidly into societies incapable of operating them effectively as the switch from governance by 'traditional' authorities (chiefs and the like) gave way in the 1950s to local elections and, on the eve of independence, to national level electoral politics, parliaments, ministries et al. (All of which makes the boast that the British Empire 'gave' democracy to its former colonies rather threadbare, quite apart from the fact that such claims ignore the decades of authoritarian, non-democratic rule that preceded independence).

There was insufficient time for 'tutelage' in the operation of the nation-state, for indigenization of bureaucracies and militaries, and whilst that was not necessarily the fault of the colonial rulers as decolonization timetables concertinaed in the 1950s, it was hardly the fault of the people residing in those colonies. Britain had only turned its hand to 'tutoring' them seriously late in the day – in the last decade of colonial rule or less. This change in policy came about when it became clear that there was little choice other than to grant colonies independence; this had not been the original mission, even though it was adumbrated in woolly rhetoric about advancement towards dominion status and eventual (the hope usually, from Britain's perspective, was for *very* 'eventual') 'self-government' *within* a British-led Commonwealth structure. Unfortunately, this tutelage usually amounted to too little, too late. Again, this was not necessarily Britain's fault; in the 1950s and 1960s, holding on to colonies became increasingly difficult. Leisurely decolonization timetables shortened dramatically, colonial nationalists bayed for independence 'now', not in a more orderly five or ten years' time, and were supported by increasingly powerful anti-colonial voices in the United Nations, the United States, and Britain's own parliament. So, suggestions such as Foreign Secretary Ernest Bevin's proposal to remain in India for an extra fifteen years to manage partition were unlikely to be taken up; nationalist politicians were not prepared to wait patiently in the wings.

Former colonies frequently achieved independence with ethnic and regional divisions firmly entrenched, limiting the chances of cross-ethnic and cross-regional identity-the main glue of successful nations-emerging. This again was a result of the speed of decolonization, which did not allow time for national institutions and identities over and above those of ethnic unit or region to develop. Colonial rule had been *based* on such divisions; whilst the 'divide and rule' jibe often leveled at British ruling techniques is wide of the mark because it disingenuously implies the deliberate and systematic creation of divisions, it was the case that British rule was based upon the maintenance and indeed the entrenchment of preexisting ones. Throughout the imperial period, the British had ruled *through* distinct ethnic and regional units—it had never, for example, ruled India, Nigeria, the Sudan, or Uganda as single units, making their fractious independence easier to understand. British rule was founded on decentralization, not the centralization required to form a successful nation-state. It is little surprise that so many of these colonies-turned-nations either struggled or failed, and were soon hijacked by corrupt elites, usually involving men that the British had groomed as their successors. Colonies were *never intended to be* nation-states, and so the quick about-turn that was at the heart of rapid decolonization meant that new nations, though possessed of the trappings of nationhood—newly built parliaments, new national anthem, flag, and independence stadium—did not have its essence or its substance. They were also bequeathed crushing economic problems associated with monocrop economies. What is more, because of the intrusion of colonialism, none of these societies had had the chance to develop its own form of statehood, and negotiate its own entry into the emerging world order. Whilst some would say there is no point crying over spilt milk, these are important facts to be considered when attempting to assess the post-independence trajectory of former colonies.

Legacies in Britain and the colonies

Legacies of the British Empire include cricket and a host of other games (polo, football, racquet sports, snooker), taken to the far corners of the earth by British soldiers and settlers. There are then the Anglicized place names and street names that pepper the former colonial world (Queen Elizabeth Land was created in Antarctica in 2012), the rich architectural heritage associated with the colonial built environment, along with driving on the right-hand side of the road, parliamentary politics, judges wearing wigs in court, and variations of the English language. Many global organizations have imperial roots, including the dense network of clubs sharing reciprocal arrangements, multinational companies, and the Boy Scouts movement. The Anglican church has more of its *c.* 85 million members in Africa than in Britain, and its thirty-eight provinces neatly map the former imperial world. Physical infrastructure, townscapes and patterns of urban segregation and zoning, are lasting legacies that continue to shape the everyday world as experienced by hundreds of millions of people. To this should be added the Empire's lasting impact on the natural world, the demarcated farmlands, forests, game reserves and imported pasturelands and species of flora and fauna. A key political legacy, still a force in the international system and viewed as a boon by its member states (particularly the smaller ones) is the modern day Commonwealth of Nations, headed by the British monarch.

Imperial legacies and continuities can also be measured by the still extensive 'kith and kin' ties linking Britain and (in particular) the former dominions, as well as the abnormally large size of British expatriate communities in places such as the Gulf states and Singapore. There are then the patterns of settled racial demographics, including people of British stock in Central and Southern Africa, Indians in Fiji and Trinidad, Afro-Caribbeans and South Asians in Britain, and the distinctive Welsh community in Argentina.

As well as its racial composition, Britain's status as a major legatee of the British Empire is manifest in other ways. These include its status as a uniquely globalized economy, its trading strength, and the position of the City of London as one of the world's major financial centres. Britain's former status as a great imperial power is also reflected in its significant political reach in terms of its diplomatic network and membership of key international bodies such as the UN Security Council. Britain's status as a living legacy of empire is also manifest in its multi-ethnic population, and in London, both as an imperial capital and a financial centre, and its monarchy and elaborate state pageantry. Legacies remain in the attitude of many people to Britain's 'place in the world', its overseas investment portfolio, and the British diaspora of over ten million people spread around the world. It is manifest in its maintenance of a military that still prides itself on a capacity to deliver 'global reach' and to act as a 'force for good' (the British military's unofficial slogan) in the world. The British armed forces recruit an increasing number of service personnel from Commonwealth countries and retain, in the Brigade of Gurkhas, a remnant of the old Indian Army.

Debates about Britain's place in the world often reflect angst regarding post-war 'decline' and the realities of the relatively sudden collapse of an enormous imperial system. It is clear that government ministries such as those responsible for defence, foreign affairs, and overseas aid, take the issue of Britain's world role very seriously. Vestiges of empire can be detected in the still strong belief that Britain has a mission to make the world a better place. This involves seeking to reform overseas societies and their institutions, an impulse implanted at the heart of British foreign policy. Be it in a foreign policy centred on 'nation-building' in the developing world or military deployments, more than a shadow of the Victorian 'civilizing mission' still exists in Britain. More than simple 'legacies' of the British Empire are the handful of colonies that Britain still possesses. Known as crown colonies until as late as 1981 though now called overseas territories, their total population exceeds a quarter of a million people. Small though they are, these remaining colonies can cause big political headaches; Anglo-Spanish relations are coloured by the issue of Gibraltar's sovereignty, and although officially part of the United Kingdom, for some people Northern Ireland remains rightfully a part of a sovereign Irish state. At the time of writing, political tension

Britain's remaining colonies in 2013

Ascension, Anguilla, Bermuda, British Antarctic Territory, British Indian Ocean Territory, the British Virgin Islands, the Cayman Islands, Cyprus Sovereign Base Areas, the Falklands, Gibraltar, Montserrat, Pitcairn, St Helena, South Georgia, the South Sandwich Islands, Tristan da Cunha, and the Turks and Caicos Islands.

between Argentina and Britain over the sovereignty of the Falklands is mounting, and foreign direct investment in the British Virgin Islands lags only slightly behind inward investment into Britain itself, part of a network of offshore jurisdictions that provide much of the 'back office' for global capitalism.

Psychological legacies

As well as the tangible legacies of the British Empire, and the traceable historical roots of current situations that were influenced by colonial rule, there are less tangible ones too. These include the psychological costs of colonialism, which are often difficult for the people of the former metropole to understand, and consequently easy to overlook or underplay. 'Perhaps you need to have been on the side of the colonized', mused Ranajit Guha, 'in order to feel the whip.' Having one's culture demeaned and repeatedly being told that European culture was superior, and having the colour of your skin debar you from equality, were exceedingly debilitating aspects of imperialism and Western dominance. That most hardy of imperial falsehoods—that if a person adopted British ways they would be treated as equal—was one of the most pernicious aspects of imperialism. The very fact of colonial status, even decades after the event, remains a burden to some people, particularly those of elite status. 'Whenever I read or hear the phrase colonial India', wrote Guha, 'it hurts me. It hurts like an injury that has healed and yet still retains some trace of the original pain.'

It has been argued that the minds of British people were 'colonized' in a variety of ways, and according to Stephen Howe we are only now going through the process of 'decolonizing the mind'. 'Four hundred years of conquest and looting', wrote Salman Rushdie, 'four centuries of being told that you are superior to the Fuzzy-Wuzzies and the wogs, leave their stain. This stain has seeped into every part of the culture, the language and daily life; and nothing much has been done to wash it out.'

Auditing the British Empire

Identifying legacies of the British Empire is a relatively straightforward task. It is far less easy to make judgements about the Empire's effects and to conduct moral and political audits or 'cost-benefit' analyses. Some imperial historians caution against chewing on the 'old chestnut' of empire good or bad (including one of the reviewers of this book at its proposal stage). Lynda Colley counsels against it too, because evidence can be found on both sides in such abundance. So do John Darwin and Ronald Hyam, other weighty names in the study of British imperialism. Serious historians of empire, they seem to argue, should steer clear of this debate. But the question cannot be sidestepped, especially in an introduction to the British Empire written for readers who might ponder this very question and consider it the most important of them all. Furthermore, historians need to engage in the debate lest it become the exclusive preserve of those who wish to score political points or peddle lightweight learning. Remaining aloof is no good at all, even if it grates on the historian's cherished pursuit of objectivity. The historian of the British Empire need not take part in point scoring; his or her role is to aid understanding of what took place, and this in turn illuminates the roots of present day situations. This is more important than compiling Britain's 'crime sheet' and apportioning blame on the one hand, or seeking to trumpet the Empire's achievements and stroke British pride on the other. When studying significant phenomena, it is natural to attempt to construct a balance sheet, and curious people will always seek to know what were the positive and negative elements of important things in order to form a basis for judgement. In the case of the British Empire, it is so often the cause of debate, and the commonest manner in which the imperial past enters the British media. Even if it can be said that the processes that constitute imperialism are part of human existence, and that the British Empire was merely a manifestation of these processes, this does not mean that its impact for good or ill is unworthy of consideration.

In attempting to build a positive picture of British imperial achievements, the intensely problematic roots of empire and its fundamental imbalances and injustices are often overlooked, perhaps because of the strong preference in parts of the world *not* subjected to imperialism to minimize the importance of this issue. But a history involving violence, dispossession, and even atrocity cannot be abridged in the rush to start telling the 'good news' story about railways and the global economy. Of course, one would not wish to claim that Britain was to 'blame' for all the ills in its former colonies. That would be absurd. Taking Africa as an example, there is no doubt that it has been atrocious, venal, often murderous African leadership since decolonization that has accounted for many of the continent's ills. But the state apparatus that Africa's leaders struggled to operate, or hijacked for their own malfeasant purposes, is a key aspect of the colonial legacy—as are patrimonial, oligarchic, undemocratic, authoritarian political structures and an international system still dominated by astonishing global inequalities often brokered by Western imperialism. So, too, are specific challenges, such as the legacy of land alienation in societies where most of the fertile land was reserved for the minority white population. Moreover, phenomena such as post-war development economics were instruments of domination created by, among other factors, the British Empire. Things are very tangled, and this illustrates why we need to ask questions and probe the historical record in order to form sustainable opinions.

Whilst the question 'what did the Romans ever do for us?' provided Monty Python with a classic comedy moment, it is a pointless historical exercise when it comes to considering British imperialism, because it is not a competition to audit the good versus the bad in order to see who wins. Furthermore, it is impossible to know what 'might have been' without the British Empire. Would lands that became colonies have 'developed' themselves, like Japan, or fallen prey to other imperial powers? We will never know. Listing the boons of empire presents an

14. Tamil tea pickers work on the Melfort Tea Estate between Kandy and Nuwara Eliya in Sri Lanka (photographed: 30 March 1996). Women plucking tea was a staple of nineteenth century adverts for tea, and remains common in today's television adverts for 'fair trade' produce

unbalanced picture because it assumes that things had to change throughout the world, and fails to take into account the 'good' things, in terms of governance, education, peace-making and so on, that were in place *before* the British arrived. On the other side of the debate, listing alleged British perfidies is also unrewarding. The risible fiction that this concocts, of a pre-colonial 'Merrie Africa' flowing with milk and honey and populated by beneficent rulers and their happy people until ruined by imperial intrusions, is equally as inaccurate. Such accounts magnify British 'crimes' and forgive everyone else their trespasses. The assailants of the imperial record naively divide the colonial world into active oppressors and passive victims, too binary a picture that ascribes far too much power to the one side and not nearly enough (if any) to the other. This rendition ascribes power to 'imperialists' that most could only have dreamed of, and assumes their consistent ill intent. It gives no credence to the ingenuity and resistance of 'the colonized' and the extent to which they were able to shape the colonial encounter. It fails to account for the strength of indigenous cultures, few of which were simply steamrollered by colonialism even if they were influenced in significant ways by it. One needs only look at the vibrant, and distinctly 'native' cultures that litter the former colonial world to appreciate the strength of indigenous culture and the limits of colonial encroachment. The 'weren't the British bastards' school of history also ignores the complicity of indigenous people in the evils of the colonial world—the African slave hunters and sellers, the Asian ethnic persecutors, the non-European thirst for the firearms that Europeans traded, -as well as any benefits bestowed.

The past, of course, is a foreign country where they do things differently. Whilst there is no sense in judging people of the past by today's standards, the *difference* in those standards illustrates key ways in which the world has changed and illuminates important attitudes and occurrences that defined empire. It can hardly be denied, for instance, that the colonial world was predicated upon inequality, and that it placed less value on the life of non-white people than white people. No one can ever 'make up for, or explain away, the evil of slavery, nor bring back to life peoples wiped out by the murder, warfare, and disease associated with European rule. The passage of time does not alter historical fact (not, of course, that people in Britain today should be guiltily apologizing). It is important to acknowledge that one's view of the British Empire depends on one's vantage point—and the vantage point at the receiving end should be considered every bit as significant as that of the armchair viewers back at home.

'Must the British Empire really be depicted', Andrew Roberts asks (quoting Priyamvada Gopal), 'as a tale of "slavery, plunder, war, corruption, exploitation, indentured labour, impoverishment, massacres, genocide, and forced resettlement", or could some objectivity be re-injected into the debate?' Well, frankly, yes it must. After listing such a catalogue of ills (though not denying them) this call for 'objectivity' is puzzling. What are we to do? Throw cricket and the English language into the balance to cancel out genocide and slavery, and call it a draw? Surely it is appropriate to avoid endorsing past actions that we would utterly disapprove of today: we would no longer consider it acceptable to take over someone else's land or kill them—so why endorse what stemmed directly from such actions in the past?

Arrogant complacency is sometimes implicit in arguments that centre upon the alleged benefits bequeathed by empire: when it is claimed, for example, that empire 'gave' the world the English language. As if it was anyone's to give or to withhold! Colonial people *took* the language, for their own reasons, in order to better themselves and seek accommodation in an unequal world, and to take advantage of opportunities. A related claim is that British imperialism 'made' (say) modern India, a sweeping contention that ignores the integral role played by Indians in the creation of their own state. This is a legacy of the lengthy period in which Westerners believed that they were in a position to command the world, and that only their agency mattered. E. H. Carr, working for the Foreign Office during the Treaty of Versailles negotiations, criticized his colleagues for supporting Russian overrule of small neighbouring states such as Latvia.

> The gist of the argument as to the small nationalities seems to be
> that someone else (i.e. Russia) is in a better position to judge what
> is good for them than they are themselves. This is a time-honoured

argument for 'benevolent' autocracy as against democracy, and for imperialism against the principle of nationality.

There are no absolutes in such a debate, reflecting the fact that there were no absolutes in terms of historical experience: some people, not all of them white, benefited from the numerous ingredients that went into making the British Empire. People were freed from slavery or protected from it; sick people were cured and some endemic diseases eradicated; mortality rates tended to drop in the long term; administrative and legal norms affecting people's lives were in some cases improved; Egyptian antiquities were preserved and railways constructed. But on the other hand, slaves were shipped from Africa; diseases of man and beast were introduced; people died, sometimes in prodigious numbers, at the hands of colonists and soldiers; functioning systems of governance and jurisdiction were skewed or destroyed; food self-sufficiency was wiped out, sometimes leading to famine; and buildings and artefacts were destroyed or looted. The paradoxes of empire abound, to the point of schizophrenia. In making any assessment, development must be weighed against de-industrialization and dependency; rights denied against rights championed; trusteeship and the desire to protect and 'uplift' natives against the growing autonomy of settler societies founded upon their dispossession and decline. Frequently, it was a case of two steps forward, three steps back. Few of the Empire's boons were unalloyed, even fewer of them were invited by the indigenous people upon whom they were visited, and the plunder and violence involved in empire is difficult to overlook even if some would prefer to forget.

In offering an assessment of the empire good or bad debate, Piers Brendon identifies a 'white gleam' and a 'red gleam'. The white gleam emphasizes the British Empire as a liberal empire, certainly when compared to some of its contemporaries. It tried to eradicate practices that (in the minds of most people) were barbaric, such as cannibalism, foot binding, and widow burning (though it should be pointed out that this on its own was not the main purpose of the British Empire, even if it might have been the main purpose of some of those who operated within it). It attempted to bring justice to common people, it undertook public works for their benefit, it led the way in abolishing the slave trade (of which, illustrating the deep ambiguities of imperial history, it had previously been the biggest practitioner). One of its central ideas was that fair and impartial rule would set people free, but not free in the sense of ordering and running their own political affairs. They needed tutelage to reach this point. Empire took British culture, language, technology, ideas of democracy, good governance, free speech, sport, fair play, enlightened values, and Christian civilization to many parts of the world. The trouble with all of this is that there was too much hypocrisy involved, including the operation of the glass ceiling that prevented 'loyal', educated, and Anglicized non-whites from being admitted to the highest levels of government and administration within the Empire. When it comes to the 'red gleam', whilst the sun never set on the British Empire, as the Chartist Ernest Jones observed, 'the blood never dried'. Empire's fundamental purpose was to increase the wealth and power of British people. 'It caused famine and despoliation. It presided over genocide and random acts of violence, dispossession, alienation, and cultural vandalism.'

As well as a tendency towards non sequiturs, defenders of the imperial record often evince an unquestioning acceptance of the Empire's own justifications, not least that British rule brought peace—the vaunted 'pax Britannica'. 'Peace' it might have brought, but in many places only after violent subjugation—and what kind of peace is that? Furthermore, endorsements of imperial achievement often rest on the laconic argument that, overall, British imperialism was a beneficent force, but that of course there were some bad things and some people suffered. Sotto voce, this argument is saying 'you can't make an omelette without breaking eggs', a perspective that understandably angers those who experienced colonialism in a bad way. Pointing to the benign district commissioners of the late colonial period misses the point about the foundations of the system they inherited, and the fundamental inequities of colonialism. Beneficial results of British imperial expansion should not be hijacked by those seeking to build an argument about the British Empire being a 'good thing' overall. Why? Because very often such 'benefits' were either *unintentional*, or were not as beneficial as is claimed. The British did not build railways in India, for example, in order to help Indians or to nurture a future independent Indian state. They did it for their own strategic and economic purposes, sometimes using forced labour, and many Indians died in the process. The fact that Indians benefited from transport links designed to ease the movement of raw materials and troops, and that now the Indian state benefits, is a subsidiary factor (and some Indians would claim that the railways bequeathed by the British featured obsolete rolling stock and had suffered from chronic under-investment). And, as Nehru once asked, did it really require 300 years of British rule in order to implant this benefit? Is it beyond the whit of man to imagine that Indian rulers might have been able to develop such technological advances themselves, or import them of their own volition?

There are a number of other common positions assumed by those seeking to argue that the British Empire was a good thing. One is that it was better than the other empires on offer. In some ways, it was – certainly better than the more murderous regimes of King Leopold of the Belgians or Germany's brief essay in African colonialism. But it is a strange, even desperate argument to forward, a sort of retrospective national competition about whose empire was least genocidal or built most roads, and rather like an argument for bragging rights between a rapist and a murderer. Another common position features the deployment of the 'they want us back' argument. What this canard fails to acknowledge is that those Sierra Leoneans, say, or Jamaicans, who make such comments—'we wish the British were still ruling us'—might just be being polite. More seriously, the argument lacks traction because it fails to understand the nature of current situations that are likely to elicit such comments. Hankering after a 'better' past is a very human trait. What is more, often the cause of the contemporary ills that such people seek refuge from are to a large extent a *result* of the colonial period and its messy conclusion, as well as global economic forces. Finally, this argument, even when it does have some measure of credibility (once established, British rule did trail peace in its wake, though it was often peace based on the employment of violence and maintained by the threat of further violence) is not a clincher for colonialism; just because something in the past (British rule) is considered better than the present does not automatically justify the former and allow its many problems to be discounted.

In debates about the positive and negative effects of imperialism an important chronological point is often overlooked. Those who claim that the British Empire was a net 'good' for the former colonies and the world in general are really referring to the *latter-day empire*. This was a period which was more benign than earlier ones, more enlightened, more developmental, less (but still overwhelmingly) racially divided, more paternalistic. But the evolution of a more benign imperialism in the twentieth century, predicated upon subjugation achieved, does not erase from the imperial escutcheon the stain of slavery, thieving settlers, or disease. Nor does it allow us to sidestep the fact that many of the Empire's alleged 'wins' were actually based upon wonky prognoses of the problems. For example, colonial officials identified soil erosion and desertification as major threats to African agriculture and ecology, attributing it to poor African farming techniques. But colonial land policies, which in some parts of Africa crowded people and their livestock into 'reserves' characterized by poor quality and insufficient land whilst appropriating fertile land for settlers, were an integral part of the problem too. This was a classic case of colonial know-how identifying the speck in one's brother's eye without noticing the rafter in one's own.

Who can honestly say that they are in a position to claim with confidence whether generations of Indians benefited from 300 years of British rule, or to disentangle the 'good' from the 'bad' in Britain's thousand-year affair with Ireland? History should not be dragooned into the service of spurious claims about the past or to celebrate suspect advantages, or on the other hand to damn as monsters men and women who sought to improve or save lives—as if anything as complex as an empire spread across the world could ever be reduced to a few sound-bites regarding railways, the rule of law, slavery, or capitalist extraction.

Empires are, by nature, exploitative. Sometimes, perhaps, exploitative in ways not deleterious to the interests of the colonized, but they exist so that the colonizer accrues benefits, be it land for settlers, smokable tobacco, more Christian converts, or dollar-earning exports. Colonial rule, as Anthony Hopkins reminds us, was 'a foreign imposition lacking popular legitimacy', a global transgression of other people's independence. The main aim of many imperial actors was to profit themselves, *not* to provide uplifting tutelage for indigenous peoples, whatever arguments were used to justify things and no matter how much the colonialists came to believe their own hype. It used widely to be claimed by European farmers and plantation owners that by the mere fact of working for them in poorly paid positions, the 'natives' benefited. This is clearly nonsense, and it is important to avoid being roped in by the justificatory hyperbole that imperialists promulgated and often ardently believed. Even in the late colonial period, the British government's concerns about national prestige and national gain dictacted approaches to decolonization every bit as much as concerns for the welfare of colonial peoples. Empire was primarily about self-interest, its purpose, in Lord Derby's words, to 'occupy, fortify, grab and brag'. The prosperity of the West was in large measure attained at the expense of groups deemed different and inferior, and empire did little to ameliorate this bedrock of inequality. The international system in which former colonies now struggle for any measure of power, the most lasting legacy of the colonial period, is similarly unequal and exploitative. That might just be 'the way it is' for humankind, but that does not mean it should be welcomed.

Jomo Kenyatta wrote that 'Africans are not hostile to European civilization as such, they would gladly learn its techniques and share in the intellectual and material benefits which it has the power to give. But they are in the intolerable position when the European invasion destroys the very basis of their old tribal way of life, and yet offers them no place on the new society except as serfs doomed to labour for bare existence'. Twenty years later, Nelson Mandela articulated the powerful and universal appeal of freedom—and what awaited those (such as colonial powers) who denied it: 'During my lifetime I have dedicated myself to this struggle of the African people. I have fought against white domination, and I have fought against black domination. I have cherished the ideal of a democratic and free society in which all persons live together in harmony and with equal opportunities. It is an ideal which I hope to live for and to achieve. But if needs be, it is an ideal for which I am prepared to die.'

Whatever its faults, Niall Ferguson writes, the British Empire 'fostered globalization, overseas investment and free trade and—in the long run—this raised levels of prosperity all round'. 'Possibly so', writes Lynda Colley, unconvinced.

But individual human beings do not live by the free market alone and nor do they live in the long run. The immediate impact of British imperial free-trading was often the collapse of local indigenous industries which were in no position to compete, and a consequent destruction of livelihoods and communities. This points to the tension at the heart of empire. Its exponents may seek (as many Britons genuinely did) to make the world a better place, but they also wanted to dominate. The Victorians wanted to spread the gospel of free trade, but they also wanted to continue being the premier workshop of the world.

The two were always mutually exclusive; empires are not for equals.

Whilst it might be possible to reach general agreement on the (by today's standards) self-serving and exploitative motives for creating the British Empire, its impacts were almost infinite, the ways in which it 'played out' diverse and often far less binary than any 'colonizer versus colonized' dichotomy can capture. Separating the 'good' elements from the 'bad' is possible, however, and this account leans towards the latter in concluding that the benefits of empire applied to fewer people than did the damage and distortion it caused, though it impinged lightly upon the lives of more people than those it tangibly benefited or tangibly disadvantaged. Measuring the British Empire is also a time-sensitive activity; whilst it is possible to identify some easy 'winners' and 'losers', it is only the passage of time, and a more Olympian view of history, that makes certain things clear. These include the fascinating possibility that empires are potentially more effective protectors of minorities and the management of religious differences than the nation-state has so far proven to be. It is also important to consider 'the British Empire' as itself a symptom of global economic change, not a cause, which diminishes its significance and leads one to ponder the imponderably counterfactual 'what might altenatively have happened' question.

Whilst focusing on the history and legacies of the British Empire, it is important not to lose sight of the wood for the trees. The significance of this one, albeit vast, empire must not obscure the facts of much wider imperialisms—at the global level right down to the level of regions and villages—and of their continuation to this day. We cannot afford to fixate on the British Empire lest this allow it to appear too monolithic, or to become a panacea for all the world's ills, historically or in the present day. The British Empire was an expression of the history of humankind.

Conclusion

For now, the impact of the British Empire still lies heavily about us, and it might be argued that the British Empire's history per se is less important than the British Empire's *impact on world history*. If we see a continuum, we can move meaningfully beyond the 'final page in the imperial epic' and still find a contemporary role for historians of Britain's interaction with the wider world (which is what imperial history has always been about). Considering Britain and the world today brings us back to the meaning of 'imperialism'. With global activity on the part of multinational companies and political departments, a smattering of overseas territories, and military deployments in Afghanistan, Iraq, Libya, Northern Ireland, and Sierra Leone, one can ask if Britain is still 'imperial' in any way. Despite the fact of Britain's alleged withdrawal from east of Suez in the late 1960s and early 1970s, supposedly a definitive 'end of empire' moment, Britain has deployed more firepower in the region in the last twenty years than it did even during the heyday of empire.

Probing the character, actions, and limitations of the 'fragmented colossus' that was the British Empire remains a richly rewarding form of historical enquiry, as well as being crucial to understanding the modern world. Whilst the 'assumed stability of colonial rule' can be challenged to present 'a picture of the British Empire as an ultimately precarious, shifting, and unruly

15. A woman walks past an Irish republican mural in west Belfast, Northern Ireland, Wednesday, 4 October 2006. A reminder of Britain's nearest colonial situation, English colonization of its neighbour dates back to the thirteenth century and, though much more stable in the past decade, remains unresolved

formation...quite distinct from its self-projected image as an orderly entity', the tangibility of Britain's presence in scores of today's nation-states was a more remarkable fact than the inevitable contradictions and weaknesses inherent in such an enormous, Heath Robinson-esque edifice.

Whilst the era of large territorial empires has passed, during which a third of the world's surface and over a third of its population were ruled by Western nations, the processes of human interaction and the economic forces that shape them do not change. Imperialism in some form will always be with us. Human beings and the communities that they form have constantly sought to influence and even to subjugate and dispossess their fellows, for different reasons, each the parent of its own rhymes of intellectual and spiritual justification. Some scholars have argued that imperialism is no longer the preserve of any one nation, but of a conglomeration of all states, corporations, the media, and culture. Millions of people continue to live in a state of dispossession and dependency. 'The wretched of the earth' are still with us, as are ruling mentalities, the globalization that European, particularly British, imperialism, fostered, and the legacies of centuries of unequal interaction between the Western and the non-Western worlds. There is controversy regarding the gap between the 'West and the Rest' and how far it can be attributed to Western imperialism. Some argue that the West systematically underdeveloped the world, others that it was an extant imbalance that made colonialism possible in the first place. Today, whilst the phenomena that the words 'empire' and 'imperialism' define are almost universally frowned upon, they still exist, whatever we choose to call them. The repression of the Kurds by various states can be viewed through the lens of imperialism. China remains an empire as much as a nation-state, and pursues policies in places such as Tibet, Africa, and the South China Sea that are reminiscent of European colonialism of old. European nations still rule a surprising number of overseas territories, and the European Union bears some of the hallmarks of empire, albeit in its more benign guise. Russia, meanwhile, retains its grasp on units of the former empire of 'Soviet Socialist Republics', sometimes with a distinct absence of benignity, and the existence of an American empire, in an era of 'pax Americana', is both denied and asserted in equal measure.

References and further reading

General further reading

With one exception, the focus here is exclusively on books that look at the British Empire as a whole. Those new to the subject might enjoy Jan Morris's classic *Pax Britannica* trilogy as a unique and exciting rendition of the Empire story. Elleke Boehmer's *Empire Writing* provides an excellent companion to the study of the Empire's history with its focus on imperial literature. There are any number of single-volume histories of the British Empire; classic texts have been written by David Fieldhouse, Ronald Hyam, Denis Judd, Bernard Porter and many others. Piers Brendon *The Decline and Fall of the British Empire*, Ronald Hyam *Understanding the British Empire*, and John Darwin's *The Empire Project* and *Unfinished Empire: The Global Expansion of Britain*, are state of the art. Illustrated introductions include Ashley Jackson, *Mad Dogs and Englishmen* and Ashley Jackson and David Tomkins, *Illustrating Empire*, whilst P. J. Marshall's *The Cambridge Illustrated History of the British Empire* is a more substantial work. Andrew Porter, *An Atlas of British Overseas Expansion* charts the Empire's rise and fall with maps. Books of the 'reader' variety are also useful for getting a sample of different types of empire-related writing and summary essays, such works including those edited by Sarah Stockwell, *The British Empire: Themes and Perspectives* and Stephen Howe, *The New Imperial Histories Reader*. Peter Cain and A. G. Hopkins's *British Imperialism, 1688–2000* is a masterful work. The *Oxford History of the British Empire* (general editor William Roger Louis) runs to five volumes and numerous companion volumes. It is indispensable, covering every region across the centuries and all of the subject's major themes (science, technology, Islam, Christianity, gender, environment, architecture, historiography, defence, literature), each essay providing useful 'further reading' lists. A browse through the scores of titles published in the influential Manchester University Press 'Studies in Imperialism' series offers the student of empire a sense of the incredible range of work taking place on aspects of the Empire's history, particularly its culture. David Abernethy, *The Dynamics of Global Dominance: European Overseas Empires, 1415–1980* (New Haven, CT: Yale University Press, 2002) offers a robust comparative account of the rise and the fall of the European empires, as does D. K. Fieldhouse, *The Colonial Empires: A Comparative Survey from the Eighteenth Century*. Back issues of the *Journal of Imperial and Commonwealth History* offer an excellent window upon the diverse field of British imperial history, featuring articles and helpful reviews of major books on the subject.

Preface

Ged Martin, 'Was there a British Empire?', *The Historical Journal*, xv, 3 (1972).

Introduction

Mark Frost, *Singapore: A Biography* (Singapore: Éditions Didier Millet, 2010).

Steve Grasse, *Evil Empire: 101 Ways in Which England Ruined the World* (Philadelphia, PA: Quirk Books, 2007).

Stuart Laycock, *All the Countries We've Ever Invaded: And the Few We Never Got Round To* (Stroud: The History Press, 2012).

H. W. Crocker, *The Politically Incorrect Guide to the British Empire* (Washington, DC: Regnery Publishing, 2011).

Niall Ferguson, *Empire* (Harmondsworth: Penguin, 2004).

Jean-Paul Sartre, 'Preface' to Franz Fanon, *The Wretched of the Earth* (New York: Grove Press, 2005).

Enoch Powell, *Daily Telegraph*, 1988.

Chapter 1: The red on the map

James Belich, *Replenishing the Earth: The Settler Revolution and the Rise of the Angloworld, 1780–1930* (Oxford: Oxford University Press, 2008).

John Darwin, *The Empire Project* (Cambridge: Cambridge University Press, 2011).

Martin Daunton, *Empire and Others: British Encounters with Indigenous Peoples, 1650–1800* (Philadelphia, PA: University of Pennsylvania Press, 1999).

Andrew Thompson in S. Stockwell, *The British Empire* (Oxford: Wiley-Blackwell, 2007).

Gary Magee and Andrew Thompson, *Empire and Globalization: Networks of People, Goods, and Capital in the British World, c.1850–1914* (Cambridge: Cambridge University Press, 2010).

Chapter 2: Defining empire: key characteristics

Mark Crinson, *Modern Architecture and the End of Empire* (Aldershot: Ashgate, 2003).

A. G. Hopkins, *The Future of the Imperial Past*, inaugural Cambridge lecture (Cambridge: Cambridge University Press, 1997).

Raymond Dummett, 'Africa's Strategic Minerals during the Second World War', *Journal of African History*, 26, 4 (1985).

Daniel Headrick, *The Tools of Empire: Technology and European Imperialism in the Nineteenth Century* (Oxford: Oxford University Press, 1981).

—— *The Tentacles of Progress: Technology Transfer in the Age of Imperialism, 1850–1940* (Oxford: Oxford University Press, 1988).

Ronald Hyam, *Understanding the British Empire* (Cambridge: Cambridge University Press, 2010).

Catherine Hall and Sonya Rose (eds), *At Home with the Empire: Metropolitan Culture and the Imperial World* (Cambridge: Cambridge University Press, 2006).

Bernard Porter, *The Absent-Minded Imperialists: Empire, Culture, and Society in Britain* (Oxford: Oxford University Press, 2006).

John MacKenzie, *Imperialism and Popular Culture* (Manchester: Manchester University Press, 1987).

Jomo Kenyatta, *Kenya: The Land of Conflict* (Manchester: Panaf Service, 1945).

John Darwin, *The Empire Project* (Cambridge: Cambridge University Press, 2011).

Tony Ballantyne in S. Stockwell (ed.), *The British Empire* (Oxford: Wiley-Blackwell, 2007).

Edward Said, *Out of Place* (London: Granta Books, 2000).

Stuart Ward in S. Stockwell (ed.), *The British Empire* (Oxford: Wiley-Blackwell, 2007).

Richard Grove, *Green Imperialism* (Cambridge: Cambridge University Press, 1996).

Chapter 3: Engines of expansion

James Belich, *Replenishing the Earth: The Settler Revolution and the Rise of the Angloworld, 1780–1930* (Oxford: Oxford University Press, 2008).

R. Hyam, *Understanding the British Empire* (Cambridge: Cambridge University Press, 2010).

John Seeley, *The Expansion of England: Two Course of Lectures* (London: Macmillan, 1899).

George MacDonald Fraser, *Flashman and the Mountain of Light* (London: Plume, 1992).

Bruce Collins, *War and Empire: The Expansion of Britain, 1790–1830* (London: Longman, 2010).

Jack Gallagher and Ronald Robinson, *Africa and the Victorians* (London: Palgrave Macmillan, 1982).

Andrew Porter, *Religion versus Empire?* (Manchester: Manchester University Press, 2004).

Carla Gardina Pestena, *Protestant Empire* (Philadelphia: University of Pennsylvania Press, 2009).

Philippa Levine, *The British Empire* (Harlow: Pearson Longman, 2007).

Brett Bennett and Joseph Hodge (eds), *Science and Empire* (London: Palgrave Macmillan, 2011).

G. Magee and A. Thompson, *Empire and Globalization* (Cambridge: Cambridge University Press, 2010).

Chapter 4: Rise and fall

William Roger Louis (general editor), *The Oxford History of the British Empire*, five volumes (Oxford: Oxford University Press, 2001).

Andrew Porter, *Historical Atlas of British Overseas Expansion* (London: Routledge, 1991).

Christopher Bayly, *Atlas of the British Empire* (New York: Facts on File, 1989).

Chapter 5: Writing the Empire story

G. Batho, 'From a Test of Memory to a Training for Life', in M. H. Price (ed.), *The Development of the Secondary Curriculum* (Beckenham: Croom Helm, 1986).

Antoinette Burton, *Empire in Question: Reading, Writing, and Teaching British Imperialsm* (London: Duke University Press, 2011).

Sugata Bose, *A Hundred Horizons* (Cambridge, MA.: Harvard University Press, 2009).

Linda Colley, 'What is Imperial History Now?', in David Cannadine (ed.), *What is History Now?* (New York: Palgrave Macmillan, 2004).

Eliga Gould, 'Foundations of Empire, 1763–83', in S. Stockwell (ed.), *The British Empire* (Oxford: Wiley-Blackwell, 2007).

Chapter 6: Legacies

Ranajit Guha, 'A Conquest Foretold', *Social Text*, 54 (1998).

Stephen Howe, 'When (If Ever) Did Empire End?: "Internal Decolonization" in British Culture since the 1950s', in Martin Lynn (ed.), *The British Empire in the 1950s: Retreat or Revival?* (London: Palgrave Macmillan, 2006).

Salman Rushdie, *Imaginary Homelands: Essays and Criticism, 1981–91* (London: Granta Books, 1991).

Andrew Roberts, 'A Date with History', *Literary Review* (August 2006).

E. H. Carr, minute, 4 December 1918, quoted in Keith Nielson, '"That Elusive Entity British Policy in Russia": The Impact of Russia on British Policy at the Paris Peace Conference', in Michael Dockrill and John Fisher (eds), *The Paris Peace Conference, 1919: Peace without Victory?* (Basingstoke: Macmillan, 2001).

John Newsinger, *The Blood Never Dried: A People's History of the British Empire* (London: Bookmarks, 2000).

Piers Brendon, 'A Moral Audit of the British Empire', *History Today* (October 2007).

Jomo Kenyatta, *Kenya: The Land of Conflict* (Manchester: Panaf Service, 1945).

John Darwin in S. Stockwell (ed.), *The British Empire* (Oxford: Wiley-Blackwell, 2007).

Index

JOIN OUR COMMUNITY

www.oup.com/vsi

- Join us online at the official Very Short Introductions **Facebook** page.
- Access the thoughts and musings of our authors with our online **blog**.
- Sign up for our monthly **e-newsletter** to receive information on all new titles publishing that month.
- Browse the full range of Very Short Introductions online.
- Read **extracts** from the Introductions for free.
- Visit our library of **Reading Guides**. These guides, written by our expert authors will help you to question again, why you think what you think.
- If you are a teacher or lecturer you can order inspection copies quickly and simply via our website.

Visit the Very Short Introductions website to access all this and more for free.

www.oup.com/vsi